WHAT PEOPLE ARE S.

Treasure Beneath

This is a wise book which offers a short, reliable course in theology; but more than that, it offers a lifetime's reflections on how one might live well. It is in turn moving, learned and thought provoking. It is a privilege to read, and will repay re-reading. I am delighted that through this book the depth of the author's understanding and his humanity are to be open to a much wider set of students than those he taught during his career as a teacher.

Professor Beverly Clack, Professor in Philosophy of Religion at Oxford Brookes University. Her books include *Sex and Death* (2002), with Brian Clack *Philosophy of Religion* (2008) and *Freud on the Couch* (2013)

I found Edward Walker's book clearly written, informative, and easy to read. It could be seen as an apologia for his private journey from firm belief to one of greater uncertainty in his religious quest; in this respect it echoed my own journey, and I suspect that of many others who have contributed to the emptying of the churches but have felt unhappy about joining the band of cynics who see any religious belief as a delusion. The value of this short book lies in its capacity to stimulate thought and discussion, perhaps enabling the theist and atheist to review their belief systems, and the agnostic to develop the rich ideas stemming from a less fearful uncertainty.

Dr Peter Agulnik, MBS, DPM, FRCPsych. Recently retired psychiatrist and psychotherapist working in Oxford for over 40 years.

I found this a well-written, intelligently constructed and interesting book. The author's professional background, both in the

Church and in education, has stood him in good stead. He has a flair for explaining complex ideas clearly. His conviction that society needs to reconnect with myths – and with religious faith – gives his writing its impassioned quality. It is a book that is evidently the fruit of a considerable period of reading and reflection.

Sibyl Ruth, Poet and author; reader, The Literary Consultancy, London

Treasure Beneath the Hearth

Myth, Gospel, and Spirituality Today

Treasure Beneath the Hearth

Myth, Gospel, and Spirituality Today

Edward Walker

CHRISTIAN
ALTERNATIVE

Winchester, UK
Washington, USA

First published by Christian Alternative Books, 2015
Christian Alternative Books is an imprint of John Hunt Publishing Ltd.,
Laurel House, Station Approach,
Alresford, Hants, SO24 9JH, UK
office1@jhpbooks.net
www.johnhuntpublishing.com
www.christian-alternative.com

For distributor details and how to order please visit the 'Ordering' section on our website.

Text copyright: Edward Walker 2014

ISBN: 978 1 782799 679 4
Library of Congress Control Number: 2014949214

A CIP catalogue record for this book is available from the British Library.

Design: Stuart Davies

Printed and bound by CPI Group (UK) Ltd, Croydon, CR0 4YY

We operate a distinctive and ethical publishing philosophy in all areas of our business, from our global network of authors to production and worldwide distribution.

CONTENTS

For Catherine
26 December 1933 – 8 July 2011
and with love to
Nicolas and Fiona

Man cannot approach the divine by reaching beyond the human; he can approach him through becoming human. To become human is what he, this individual man, has been created for.
Martin Buber

Christian and Human are tending no longer to coincide. In that lies the great Schism that threatens the Church.
Pierre Teilhard de Chardin

Acknowledgements

I am very grateful to all who have helped in bringing this book to birth. Ann Crane, Professor Beverly Clack and Professor Brian Clack were among the first to read and comment on an early draft; Simon Greenall and Ian Miller read part of the text of a later draft and prompted me to make some alterations. Sibyl Ruth, from The Literary Consultancy to whom I submitted the text, made some useful comments and criticisms, and encouraged me to continue the project. The Rev. Professor Dennis Nineham kindly read the manuscript and gave me the assurance that I had not misrepresented the position of modern New Testament scholarship. At a late stage Dr. Peter Agulnik read and commented on the text, and satisfied me that I had not misrepresented the findings of psychoanalysis. My son Nicolas fixed me up with internet access and generally acted as my godfather as I entered what was for me the scary world of the web. My daughter Fiona has been a wonderful support in bringing the book to publication, and with her professional skills has saved me from many a disaster. My wife Catherine steadily encouraged me over the years of the book's gestation, but sadly died three years before it appeared in print. Thank you to her, and to all.

Introduction

We have been here before, of course; lived at a time when the beliefs and structures of the old religion no longer resonated with present human experience. The Romans, and the Greeks before them, saw their gods and goddesses melt away like snowmen and their rituals turn into meaningless formalities. Now it's the turn of Christianity. At the end of the Roman era it had appeared as a new, more meaningful, way of expressing fundamental human aspirations. No longer; for most people in the West, whether they have read it or not, *The God Delusion*[1] emerges as the new scripture, brimming with words, thoughts, ideas to which they find themselves responding with a heartfelt "Yes", even if many also think that the "religion question" is not quite as clearly settled as Professor Dawkins believes it to be.

The function of the following pages is not to provide an ice-pack for the melting snowman. Candlelit carol services often fill the churches at Christmas time, and may encourage the illusion that the old religion is still alive; but empty churches during the rest of the year witness to a different reality. Wistful nostalgia indulged in once a year is no nourishment for the twenty-first-century person wanting to live out a life of integrity and purpose.

This is the kind of person to whom these pages are addressed. Wholeheartedly contemporary, she, or he, will be someone who recognises within herself not a need exactly, but something inner, living, to which she wants to attend. It has been called the search for meaning, and by the great American psychologist Rollo May "The Cry for Myth". By no means everyone will feel such a need. The author Robert Byron believed that human beings' distinction from animals lay in the former's awareness of a sense of "quest". "In some," he wrote, "the impulse is negligible. In others it dictates the whole course of existence. Of the latter there are, in the main, two sorts. There are the humanists... whose faith rests implicit in their desires... and, secondly, there are those for whom no physical interpretation... can suffice. These are the religious whose goal takes the form of God."[2]

It is as well to recognise that there are these "two sorts" (or rather three sorts, for we must include the "negligibles"), otherwise a lot of energy will be spent by one trying to persuade the other that they are wrong, and this can be as fruitless as the arguments of the Reformation. We live in a pluralist society, so it is much better for each of us to attend patiently to the convictions of others, recognising that tension can be creative. The scientist-theologian John Polkinghorne has written of the "surgical" value of the scientific discoveries of the latter half of the nineteenth century, perceived at the time to be destructive of Christian faith; surgical because in time those discoveries helped Christians to arrive at a far more profound and mature understanding of that faith. So Richard Dawkins' term "The God Delusion" may have a surgical role to play for those "whose goal takes the form of God."

The pages which follow have a twofold purpose. First, to look at the religious quest within the context of myth, to examine the role of myth, and to ponder the relation of "inner" to "outer" in human living with the help of the insights provided by psycho-analysis; second, to take a closer look at those four little writings which have become known as gospels and which date from the latter half of the first century CE to the early part of the second century. (CE – Common Era, and BCE – Before the Common Era will be used to signify dates in preference to the more restrictive terms AD and BC to which they correspond.) Because they come from a culture utterly different from our own, recourse will be had to the work of modern critical scholarship in helping us to understand them. The purpose of such study, however, is not an end in itself, it is rather to undertake what Karen Armstrong in her book *A History of God* calls "a dialogue with the past *in order to find a perspective from which to view the present(,)... a* jumping-off point which enables men and women to engage with the perennial questions about the meaning of life."[3] This aim will be spelled out more clearly in the chapter on "The Lord's Prayer".

While I have a degree in Classics and Theology, I lay no claim to expert knowledge, nor have I any expertise in the realm of depth psychology, although I have an interest in both. The first eighteen years of my career were spent as an Anglican priest, five of them in South Africa in the high noon of the *apartheid* era. Those five years affected me profoundly, and still do, in two particular ways. First, they confronted me with the tension we all experience between separateness and togetherness; second, with the possibility that "God" could indeed be delusional. White South Africa at the time was a deeply religious society, informed by a strict Calvinist ethic. Dutch Reformed churches were packed out, Sunday by Sunday, and yet they expressed a religion which underpinned *apartheid* and maintained a deeply unjust political and social system. An example of the consequences of this system struck me forcibly at the funeral of the 12-year old daughter of a Coloured (mixed race) couple. The father was an alcoholic, and ran a decrepit store in the African reserve. They had an English surname, and after the funeral the father asked me if I knew his brother, who owned a garage in the local town, and had a fine house up on the mountain. Of course, I suddenly saw it; not just the same surname, but I could see the physical resemblance, but there was no brother – or rather half-brother – at the funeral, no uncle to see his desperately poor niece lowered into the earth. Nor was it only its social and political expression which made me question outwardly flourishing religious practice; religion could also entail, I began to see, a psychological crippling, to which Laurens van der Post had drawn attention more than seventy years before. The Afrikaners' religion, he had suggested (he was himself Afrikaans), involved the projection of their own dark self upon their black fellow-countrymen; social *apartheid* was the expression of an internal *apartheid*, a denial of the coexistence within themselves of their own light-and-dark humanity.[4] Another deeply tragic incident towards the end of my time in South Africa vividly illustrated the consequences of this inner *apartheid*. The Afrikaans owner of a little café where I used to go regularly to buy his excellent little steak and kidney pies was discovered by the police in bed with an African girl. The law of the land meant imprisonment for this offence. But his own shame, and the condemnation and ostracism he faced from his fellow churchgoers were too much for him. He doused himself with petrol and lit a match. I imagined the conversations going on in those churches the following Sunday. "Have you heard…?" And I thought of that moving story in the eighth chapter of the Gospel of John. "Teacher, this woman has been caught in the act of adultery." Has not humanity got to be either all black or all white? Jesus' doodling in the sand made it clear that, no, it did not have to be. I knew nothing of the man apart from his steak pies, nothing at all of the girl. But could it be, I wondered, that in that encounter, beyond the lust and the shame, his humanity had been, or could have been, for a moment healed ? And it was not until much later that, reading the 18th chapter of the Gospel of Luke, I realised that I had a Pharisee and a Publican within myself who needed to be reconciled with one another.

Eight years after returning to Britain, and after a year's teacher training, I left the ministry to start a new career as a teacher of Religious Education in a comprehensive (i.e. non-selective) state school. Many people asked me whether I had lost my faith, but my own perception was that, as a result of various vicissitudes, I had found it; not in the sense that I had arrived (not by any means), rather that I was on a track which led far beyond the walls by which I had previously felt circumscribed. Sceptical, disenchanted, hormone-racing adolescents were, of course, a very different audience from the compliant congregations to which I had looked down from the pulpit, and my initial failures were frequent and humiliating. But gradually, and no doubt as a result of the moulding to which I was subjected by those adolescents, I came to value my new role in ways that I could not have imagined. I became grateful for the immensely moving experience of observing at close quarters the miraculous process in which rosy-cheeked children are transformed, within the space of half a dozen years, into bulgy or bristly adults who leave to go to work or university; and I came to see that I shared with my colleagues in the other departments a common goal, which could be described as fostering the humanity of our pupils. The scientists, for example, were stimulating in them the spirit of enquiry into the amazing and exciting complexities of the physical world of which they themselves were a part. The historians were encouraging them to look beyond their own limited horizons and to see themselves as part of a continuous unfolding process. The English department was fostering and provoking their astonishing gift of speech, holding up before them other paradigms of the use of their language than the limited ones of their own everyday world. All might have been saying, "You are greater than you think you are. Open your eyes to a world larger in every dimension than that of which you are at present aware." The Religious Education department was also engaged in this same process of perspective-enlargement. "The striving for a goal," Alfred Adler had written, "the purposiveness of the psyche, is not only a philosophical assumption, but a fundamental fact."[5] Seated at those desks were young people in whom, however deeply buried, was the striving for a goal, and in some of them was what Robert Byron had identified as a sense of quest. Their development depended upon their being opened to this sense of quest, to something of the forms which it had taken, and to at least a sample of those great "masters of living" in whom the sense of quest had burned brightly – the Buddha, Moses, Jesus, Mohammed. Religious Education did not seek to convert, but to educate, to evoke that goal-ward striving and to see how it might be connected with the sense of quest.

There was another way in which my time as a teacher in a comprehensive school helped to mould me. Comprehensive – that is to say all-ability – schools in Britain frequently get a bad press, and from time to time the cry is heard, "Bring back the grammar (i.e. selective) schools." What is not heard is its unspoken counterpart, "Bring back the secondary modern schools"; and perhaps this is because of some unconscious recognition that rigid separation of children at the age of eleven tended to shadow the unselected with a sense of failure or rejection. As I reflect on my own experience I feel a sense of deep gratitude for the privilege of being part of a comprehensive school. It helped to foster that glimmering awareness which my time in South Africa had given me, that for all the seemingly insurmountable problems entailed by attempts of diverse races, classes and religions to live together, this was the goal to which humanity was being called. Just occasionally I was given a vision of that goal by being part of a community of men and women, boys and girls, whose ages ranged from eleven to sixty; whose abilities ranged from the highly intelligent, future doctors and professors, to the slowest plodders for whom holding a pen or reading a book was little short of torture. Then there was the range of personalities, from the attractive to the unattractive, the eager to the stroppy, the genial to the shy and the withdrawn. It is true that that school did not include the mix of races that is found in most inner-city schools; but as far as it went, it gave me a vision of a goal worth striving for. In the high noon of mid-nineteenth-century industrial expansion one of the first wave of Christian Socialists (F.D. Maurice, or perhaps Charles Kingsley) had written, "Cooperation, not competition, is the law of the universe." This was a law which we all, teachers and pupils, had to try and learn in a society whose emphasis was far more on competition.

Religious fundamentalism, at present in the ascendant, is walled around, hostile to openness and closed to criticism. In its most strident form it takes upon itself the task of exposing what it sees as "The Science Delusion". The purpose of this book is utterly different. Its aim is to look at the life and teaching of Jesus (as decisive an influence on European culture, as the life and teaching of the Buddha has been in Thailand, or that of Mohammed in the Middle East) in the light both of modern biblical scholarship and of the insights into human living provided by depth psychology. If it can assist in the human quest, and make a contribution to the dialogue between the "nothings", the humanists and the religious, it will have fulfilled its aim.

Chapter 1

Only Connect

The Search

In answer to those who would seek wisdom anywhere but in their own religious tradition, the great Jewish philosopher Martin Buber records a tale about a poverty-stricken rabbi, Eizik of Cracow, who dreamed he would find treasure under a bridge in Prague. The rabbi set off, and when he arrived in Prague told the guard at the bridge about his dream. The guard laughed and said that he had once had a similar dream, that he should go to Cracow, to the house of one Eizik, son of Yekel, and dig for treasure under his stove. How could one follow such dreams! At once the old rabbi returned to his own home, dug beneath the stove, and found the treasure he had gone so far to seek. "Our treasure (Buber comments) is hidden beneath the hearth of our own home." [1] His tale, one of a collection of such tales coming from the Jewish mystical tradition known as Hasidism, provides a theme (and the title) for this book. By digging beneath the hearth of our own home we are not denying or diminishing the value of the treasure lying beneath the hearths of others, any more than we should be demeaning the history and language of other peoples by giving time to the study of our own. Whether we like it or not, it is through Christianity that what Jung called the "primordial images" (i.e. our culture's religious language) have been transmitted. Our culture, that is to say, is Judaeo-Christian, not Buddhist or Islamic.

It was in the death camp of Auschwitz that another great Jewish doctor and thinker, Viktor Frankl, found himself reflecting profoundly on the condition of twentieth-century humankind. How could the heirs of the Enlightenment, the fellow-citizens of Luther, Bach and Beethoven, have come to such a pass that they should seek to exterminate millions of their own people? And how could the victims of that inhumanity somehow preserve their own humanity without surrendering to hatred or despair? There were, he felt, two potentialities within everyone. "Man is that being who has invented the gas chambers of Auschwitz; however, he is also that being who has entered those gas chambers upright, with the Lord's Prayer or the *Shema Yisrael* on his lips."[2] He realised, moreover, that "if common values and meanings are to be found, another step must be taken, thousands of years after mankind developed monotheism, the belief in the one God. Monotheism is not enough; it will not do. What we need is not only belief in the one God but also awareness of the one mankind, the awareness of the unity of humanity. I would call it 'mon-anthropism'."[3]

Both Reason and Religion can be perverted, with disastrous results; both can foster or prevent the realisation of *monanthropism*. The Rationalism that spread so rapidly from the second half of the nineteenth century was an inevitable response to the obscurantism of the religious, and this may help to explain why Sir James Frazer, famous author of *The Golden Bough: A Study in Magic and Religion*, dismissed myth (the language of religion) as "the mistaken explanations of phenomena, whether of human life or of external nature. Such explanations originate in that instinctive curiosity concerning the causes of things which at a more advanced stage of knowledge seeks satisfaction in philosophy and science, but being founded on ignorance and misapprehension they are always false."[4] Freud, born a couple of years after Frazer, was equally insistent that it was an illusion "to suppose that what science cannot give us we can get elsewhere."[5]

Side by side with this hard "realist" approach, however, is another whose roots go back to the Romantic Movement. The Russian philosopher Nicolas Berdyaev, writing twelve years after the completion of Frazer's *Golden Bough*, deplored the habit of "identifying myth with invention, with the illusions of primitive mentality, and with anything, in fact, which is essentially opposed to reality." On the contrary, he maintained, "the creation of myths among people denotes a real spiritual life, more real, indeed, than that of abstract concepts and of rational thought. Myth is always concrete and expresses life better than abstract thought can do... It brings together two worlds symbolically."[6] Here we have the beginnings of the idea of the complementarity of the two worlds of intellect and imagination, and ultimately of religion and science. Nearer to the present, Theodore Roszak, one-time Professor of History at California State University, has protested at the meaninglessness of technological achievements without what he referred to as "transcendent correspondence". "They leave ungratified that dimension of the self which reaches out into the world for enduring purpose, undying value. That need is not some unfortunate psychic liability left over from the infancy of the human race which we ought now to outgrow. It is, rather, the emotional reflection in mankind of that intentional thrust we can find in the most basic organic stuff, in the purposeful protein matter that toils away in every cell of our being."[7] More recently, Karen Armstrong has expressed a similar view. "It is a mistake," she writes, "to regard myth as an inferior mode of thought, which can be cast aside when human beings have attained the age of reason. Mythology is not an early attempt at history, and does not claim that its tales are objective fact." Furthermore, she maintains, "mythology... is not about opting out of the world, but about enabling us to live more intensely within it."[8] This is an idea to which we shall be returning.

The argument here is not between Christian and sceptic, theist and atheist, nor to do with the existence or non-existence of God, with whether the creation of the world was a matter of chance or divine purpose, or whether man has, or has not, a soul. It is to do rather with a way of reflecting, like Frankl, on what it is to be human, and in the light of this what are primary and what are secondary tasks. So for Lewis Mumford "it is not in extensive cosmonautic exploration of outer space but by more intensive cultivation of the historic inner spaces of the human mind, that we shall recover the human heritage."[9] These writers are not speaking for any particular faith system or community of belief, but for a vision of humanity which in their view is in danger of being lost. In the nineteenth century, of course, it was not only Blake's "dark Satanic mills" that were depriving human beings of their heritage, but, as Marx so prophetically saw, the alliance of religion with the system which kept those mills going. "Religion is the sigh of the oppressed creature, the heart of a heartless world, just as it is the spirit of an unspiritual situation. It is the opium of the people. The abolition of religion as the illusory happiness of the people is required for their real happiness. The demand to give up the illusions about its condition is the demand to give up a condition which needs illusions."[10] The convergence with Freud is obvious. His focus, of course, was on the inner rather than the outer chains that were depriving people of real happiness, including the repressive attitude to sex which has been such a destructive element in Christian belief and practice.

The religious, then, whose goal takes the form of God, needed the cleansing vision of Marx and Freud to enable them to see a distinction which has been drawn by another of the great thinkers of the twentieth century, the German-American psychologist and philosopher, Erich Fromm. *"The question is not religion or not,"* he wrote, "but *which kind of religion,* whether it is one furthering man's development, the unfolding of his specifically human powers, or one paralysing them."[11] It is the distinction, in other words, between "authoritarian" and "humanistic" religion.

What might this humanistic (or *monanthropistic*) religion be? Is it simply a matter of doing as you would be done by, trying to live an ethical life, or is it something more? Fromm's own definition of religion is *"any system of thought and action shared by a group which gives the individual a frame of orientation and an object of devotion."*[12] As opposed to Humanism, it implies some kind of internal activity, some kind of internal dialogue with images or symbols not one's own (though not excluding one's own). It assumes that our most powerful motivations come from the heart rather than from the head; that it is in fact from imagination that action springs. And the language of the imagination, developed by and deeply imprinted in humankind in the course of its development over the millennia, is the language of myth.

The Language of Myth

In her book *The Battle for God*[13], a penetrating analysis of Fundamentalism, Karen Armstrong distinguishes between the complementary roles within human culture of what she calls "Mythos" (all that finds expression in poetry, drama, music, art, religion) and what she calls "Logos" (all that finds expression in rational argument and scientific analysis). Fundamentalism, whether in the Jewish, Christian, or Muslim cultures that she investigates, appears to be a response to a situation in which value has been accorded to "Logos" alone, and in which "Mythos" has been disparaged. It is the child, in fact, of a modern, materialistic mindset, which, in the words of the great Protestant scholar John Hick, has "so restricted us to the alternatives of straight fact or straight fiction that we find it difficult to feast on poetry, allowing emotion free rein, rejoicing in the magical powers of the imagination, and glorying in a great mythic story as our human way of relating to that which transcends all human thought."[14] Seen as a fight to the death, it ends up with death, in the twin towers of New York or on the streets of London, Madrid or Moscow. So it is of the utmost importance that the religious free themselves from this "either-or" mentality, and acknowledge the truth of Hick's observation, that religious experience "can express not only an openness, but also a closedness, to the Divine, and a closedness that is all the more dangerous for being expressed religiously."[15]

Reference has already been made to Richard Dawkins' *The God Delusion*. In another book, *Unweaving the Rainbow* [16], a wonderful celebration of the "poetry" of science, Dawkins uses some words of Jawaharlal Nehru, independent India's first Prime Minister, to underline his own conviction of the overwhelming importance of science in the modern world. "It is science alone that can solve the problems of hunger and poverty, of insanitation and illiteracy, of superstition and deadening custom and tradition, of vast resources running to waste, of a rich country inhabited by starving people. Who indeed could afford to ignore science today? At every turn we have to seek its aid... The future belongs to science and those who make friends with science."[17] It is in no sense to deny or belittle Nehru's words to suggest that it might also be worth attending to the words of another great Indian, Mohandas Gandhi, Nehru's one-time mentor and later (when Nehru diverted a significant proportion of India's scant resources to the military defence of Kashmir against the wishes of its Muslim majority) severe critic. "Political education is nothing worth," wrote Gandhi in 1946, "if it is not backed by a sound grounding in religion; by which is not meant sectional or sectarian belief. Man without religion is man without roots. Therefore religion is the basis on which all life structure has to be erected, if life is to be real."[18] Might it be possible not to have to choose between Nehru and Gandhi, but to plead the cause both of intellect and imagination, of the balancing of discursive reason by the wisdom of the unconscious?

It must be recognised at the outset that if intellect unbalanced by imagination can become sterile, imagination unbalanced by intellect can become fantasist. Imagination can be used not only for creative, life-affirming ends but also as a means for escaping from the hard realities of life. For the imagination's capacity to create illusory satisfactions Freud found plenty of evidence in his consulting room. "At the time when the development of the sense of reality took place," he wrote in 1930, "this region (i.e. imagination) was expressly exempted from the demands of reality-testing and was set apart for the purpose of fulfilling wishes which were difficult to carry out." Religious needs derived, in Freud's view, from the infant's sense of helplessness and consequent longing for the father. Religious practice was "the attempt to procure a certainty of happiness and a protection against suffering through the delusional remoulding of reality"; a process, he remarks, which "presupposes an intimidation of the intelligence," and condemns human beings to remain in a state of "infantilism".[19]

Religious fundamentalism, with its refusal, for example, to acknowledge the clear evidence provided by fossils, plainly does involve an intimidation of the intelligence. However, Marion Milner, a British analyst in the Freudian tradition but of a later generation, has suggested that imagination, while undoubtedly it could and did serve to exercise an escapist function, could also be used as "a way of thinking about hard facts, as an instrument, not for evading the truth, but for reaching it."[20]

The time may now have arrived when there is the possibility of rehabilitating myth and recognising it as a deeply creative product of the imagination, rich with the possibility of enhancing life and comprehending reality. So, certainly, it appeared to Rollo May, for whom the reinstatement of myth was one of the most urgent needs of our time. "Many of the problems of our society," he writes, "including cults and drug addiction, can be traced to the lack of myths which give us as individuals the inner security we need to live adequately in our day. The sharp increase in suicide among young people and the surprising increase of depression among people of all ages are due… to the confusion and the unavailability of adequate myths in modern society."[21] An analyst of deep wisdom and long experience, he would have nothing to do with a simplistic "return to religion," but held that human beings' "cry for myth" was as fundamental as their cry for food. In fact it is no accident that the emergence of the psychoanalytic movement coincided not only with the rapid erosion of and sense of connection with religious belief and practice, but also with the beginning of an age in which humanity's long preoccupation with food had finally (in the West) become satisfied, and a further need had become apparent. "We could define psychoanalysis," writes May, "as the search for one's own myth."[22]

The recognition of this search, and of the healing quality of myth, is not new. "Society, without knowing it, is *starving* for the inner," we find the maverick Scottish psychiatrist R.D. Laing writing some fifty years ago. "The outer, divorced from any illumination from the inner is in a state of darkness."[23] Passionately opposed to any form of psychotherapy, whether in the form of drugs or counselling, which ignores this inner need and views its task as assisting the "patient" back to "normality", Laing pleads for a true "soul-healing" which would enable people to find within themselves an "orientation in the geography of inner space and time."[24] This is a hard task for a culture which has shifted, in Don Cupitt's phrase, "from myths to maths"[25]. In contemporary usage myth has come to signify fantasy and untruth, something which according to Frazer is founded on ignorance and misapprehension. At the same time it is easy to see what brought about the devaluing of myth. After the terrible religious conflicts of the sixteenth and seventeenth centuries reason and science appeared as saviours from the divisive prejudices and dogmas of the religious. Since then, however, it has come to be realised that it is not only religious conflict which has continued to disfigure the world, but the secular regimes of Hitler, Stalin and Pol Pot; and on top of these the spread of that wasteland which is the dark side of the progress of technology.

"Only connect." E.M. Forster's celebrated aphorism might

stand as a motto for all those who seek the marriage of intellect and imagination – of maths and myths. Perhaps a humble waiting upon a source of wisdom within, coming to us from strata of our evolution far below the level of consciousness, may be the indispensable condition not only for perceiving the poverties of our own culture and enriching it, but also for making possible a more open, humble approach to cultures other than our own. Jung was certainly in no doubt as to the importance of the ancient myths, common to humankind but appearing in different guises according to the different conditions imposed by time, climate and culture, "which are older than historical man… and, eternally living, outlasting all generations, still make up the groundwork of the human psyche. It is only possible (he suggests) to live the fullest life when we are in harmony with these symbols; wisdom is a return to them."[26] A similar view has been expressed by the distinguished American mythologist Joseph Campbell. Myths, he asserts, "actually touch and bring into play the vital energies of the whole human psyche. They link the unconscious to the fields of practical action, not irrationally, in the manner of neurotic projection, but in such fashion as to permit a mature and sobering, practical comprehension of the fact-world to play back, as a stern control, into the realms of infantile wish."[27] Mircea Eliade, who has probably done more than any other scholar in this field to recover appreciation of the language of myths goes further, insisting that they continue below the surface of human life, like an underground river. "They may become disguised, mutilated or degraded, but are never extirpated;"[28] and though modern man "is free to despise mythologies and theologies… that will not prevent his continuing to feed upon decaying myths and degraded images."[29]

Through the work of scholars like Eliade, Campbell, Fromm and others within the scientific community itself, we may now be beginning to move away from what E.F. Schumacher described as the age of "scientific imperialism".[30] Like the age of "theological imperialism" which preceded it, it will not disappear all at once. Both have claimed omni-competence, and both have been unwilling to acknowledge the partiality of their own perspectives and the complementarity of the other's. But the time may now be right for a reappraisal of those ancient mythologies of our own culture which have been bulldozed so rapidly from our awareness, and for considering Schumacher's proposition that "religion is the reconnection (re-ligio) of man with reality, whether this reality be called God, Truth, Allah... or Nirvana."[31]

Jung and the Religious Task

It is not the purpose of this book to press the claims of one school of psychoanalysis rather than another – or indeed to press the claims of psychoanalysis at all. It will be contended, however, that whether or not psychoanalysis can be classed as a science, it has provided valuable insights into the factors which help or hinder the development of a fully human life, helped too to expose the illusions fostered by authoritarian religion itself. If reference is made to Jung rather than to others in this field, it is because he devoted more time to the consideration of religion than others.

"Among all my patients in the second half of life," Jung famously wrote in the early 1930s, "there has not been one whose problem in the last resort was not that of finding a religious outlook on life. It is safe to say that every one of them fell ill because he had lost that which the living religions of every age have given to their followers, and none of them has really been healed who did not regain his religious outlook. This of course has nothing whatever to do with a particular creed or membership of a church."[32] It is not surprising that Jung took religion so seriously. His father had been a clergyman, and Jung had seen his father wrestle with his faith – and lose. The theological structure in which his father had been educated and which had supplied his livelihood had failed him (Jung felt) in his hour of need, because while it had given him *beliefs* it had not given him *experience of God*. Some idea of how Jung understood his father's predicament may be gained from words he wrote nearly fifty years after his father's death. "It may easily happen... that a Christian who believes in all the sacred figures is still undeveloped and unchanged in his inmost soul because he has 'all God outside' and does not experience him in his soul." What is true of the individual is true also of Christian civilisation as a whole, which (Jung went on to say) "has proved hollow to a terrifying degree; it is all veneer, but the inner man has remained untouched and therefore unchanged. His soul is out of key with his external beliefs."[33]

For this state of affairs Jung blamed the churches, in that they had failed to make a clear distinction between the literal and the mythological. It is a point he takes up in a letter written in 1952. "The insistence on the uniqueness of Christianity, which removes it from the human sphere and doesn't even allow it a mythological status conditioned by history, has... (a disastrous) effect on the layman... The gospel becomes unreal; all possible points of contact with human understanding are abolished, and it is made thoroughly implausible and unworthy of belief." The gospels' embodying of the great archetypal myths, present within the psyche long before Christianity and still active in human beings, is neglected or even denied. Yet "without this link the Jesus legend remains a mere wonder story, and is understood as little as a fairy story that merely strives to entertain."[34]

In an age of rapid change and widespread confusion, such as we are now experiencing, the claims of those who profess religious certainty have a strong appeal. The fundamentalists, or semi-fundamentalists, appear to represent the strongest religious force throughout the world today; they testify, in Karen Armstrong's phrase, to "a desire to fill the void with certainty."[35] "Mythos," instead of being regarded as complementary to

"Logos," becomes opposed to it. This process only began to occur in the period 1870-1900, when Darwin's evidence for evolution appeared to hole Christianity below the waterline. Reason was in the ascendant, and the rational basis of the modern world made it "very difficult to see truth as anything other than factual or scientific."[36] The proponents of "Creationism" or "Intelligent Design", and those who for so long resisted proposals to ordain women as priests and bishops (and those who still resist the ordination of gay clergy), reflect an attachment to an infallible scripture and an ignoring of empirical fact analogous to the attitudes of those who condemned Galileo in the seventeenth century. For many the literal historicity of the Virgin Birth and the Bodily Resurrection of Jesus fall into this same category, so that the puzzled enquirer, if, "with the limited means at his disposal, he begins to reflect on these things, ... will have to confess that he does not understand them at all and that only two possibilities are open to him: either to believe implicitly, or to reject such statements because they are flatly incomprehensible."[37] This ignores, of course, the considerable work undertaken by committed scholars (of which use will be made in the succeeding chapters) to bring into a genuine relation the "external beliefs" with the facts of experience. All too frequently, however, these efforts go unnoticed or are castigated by defenders of orthodoxy as a betrayal of the fundamentals of the faith.

The purpose of Jung's analytical psychology (as he called it) was, in his view, identical to that which in every age had been provided by religion, namely "the achievement of personality, (which) means nothing less than the best possible development of all that lies in a particular, single being."[38] The fulfilling of each person's human potential, as the open flower is the fulfilling of the potential hidden in the seed, Jung calls "individuation." It refers to the actual, concrete living out of a human life to its utmost limits. He dismisses the charge that this is a purely selfish, private goal. On the contrary, he argues, bringing to their fullest development those potentialities which lie hidden within the human species is a duty laid upon it by life. He welcomed the work of his French contemporary, the great Jesuit priest-scientist Pierre Teilhard de Chardin, whose writings (placed on the Index during his lifetime by the authorities of the Roman Catholic Church) first began to appear in print only after his death, during the last six years of Jung's life. "It is not *well-being,*" wrote Teilhard, "but a hunger for *more-being* which, of psychological necessity, can alone preserve the thinking earth from the *taedium vitae.*"[39]

To many of course, then as now, Christianity had had its day, but not to Jung. "I am convinced that it is not Christianity, but our conception and interpretation of it that has become antiquated," he wrote. "The Christian symbol is a living thing that carries in itself the seeds of further development. It can go on developing; it depends only on us, whether we can make up our minds to meditate again, and more thoroughly, on the Christian premises."[40] Jung's concern was not to be a religious, let alone a Christian, apologist, but to do justice to the reality of human experience as he had come to know it in himself and in the very many patients who came to consult him. For him the argument between the theist and the atheist was irrelevant. "God is an obvious psychic and non-physical fact, i.e. a fact that can be established psychically but not physically."[41] For this reason he preferred to speak of the "God-image," which "does not coincide with the unconscious as such, but with a special content of it, namely the archetype of the self."[42]

Jung coined (he did not of course invent) the term Archetype to express something in human beings analogous to instincts observable in other living beings: the particular nest-building habits of weaver-birds, for example, or the flying formation of migrating geese. They are in-built, "imprinted" patterns which emerge in people from immensely different eras and cultures, clothed in different forms but nonetheless having a basic identity. The title of Joseph Campbell's book *The Hero with a Thousand Faces* refers to one such image, and in that book Campbell, echoing words of Rollo May quoted earlier, suggests the function that archetypes fulfil. "It has always been the prime function of mythology and rite to supply the symbols that carry the human spirit forward, in counteraction to those other constant human fantasies that tend to tie it back. In fact, it may well be that the very high incidence of neuroticism among ourselves follows from the decline among us of such effective spiritual aid."[43] Others have observed this same "pull" between two opposing forces within human beings, the pull between growth and stagnation, adventure and safety. We shall return to this theme later. Could it be that only the recovery of living myth can offer an alternative to those "decayed myths and degraded images" which inevitably tie the spirit back and do nothing to foster its forward urgings?

The suggestion that emerges from Jung's work is that, faced with this choice, human beings have the possibility of discovering and harnessing the life-giving, forward-pulling resources within them. This task is one aspect of that "intensive cultivation of the historic inner spaces of the human mind" for which Lewis Mumford pleads as a means of recovering "the human heritage." And just as "extensive cosmonautic exploration of outer space" requires a high degree of commitment, so does the exploration and cultivation of inner space. "The development of personality is a favour that must be paid for dearly,"[44] wrote Jung.

The Greek writer Nikos Kazantzakis, in his autobiographical *Report to Greco*, expressed this inward exploration which is at the same time a forward reaching by means of three arresting images. "I was always bewitched by three of God's creatures," he wrote, "the worm that becomes a butterfly, the flying fish that leaps out of the water in an effort to transcend its nature, and the silkworm that turns its entrails into silk." But it was the first image which he found the most compelling. "For me, the grub's yearning to become a butterfly always stood as its – and man's – most imperative and at the same time most legitimate duty."[45] Excommunicate like Tolstoy from the Orthodox Church, he yet found in the death and resurrection of Christ the ultimate symbol that gave these images their force. "Every man worthy of being called a son of man bears his cross and mounts his Golgotha. Many, indeed most, reach the first or second step, collapse pantingly in the middle of the journey, and do not attain the summit of Golgotha, in other words the summit of their duty; to be crucified, resurrected, and to save their souls. Afraid of cruci-fixion, they grow faint-hearted; they do not know that the cross is the only path to resurrection. There is no other path."[46]

The consequence of Jung's contention that there is in every human being a "God-image" beckoning towards more-being, is that for those who feel "the grub's yearning" within themselves (Roszak's "intentional thrust") some kind of dialogue with the God-image becomes imperative. Perhaps this is what is repre-sented by those ringing words of the *Shema*, the bedrock of Jewish faith: "You shall love the Lord your God with all your heart, and with all your soul, and with all your might."[47] Unless a person's whole energy is committed to this task the possibility of any real movement towards more-being is limited. Espousal of religion of course is no guarantee of this movement, as Jung had observed in the case of his clergyman father. Christianity, in spite of the passion (in both senses) of its founder, has no more escaped the straitjacket of formalism than any other great religion. That is why, in Jung's view, it had to "begin again if it is to meet its educative task," which is to enable people to experience "the divine image as the innermost possession of their own souls."[48] Beginning again, for Christianity, means first of all looking with fresh eyes at the figure of Christ as he is presented in the pages of the gospels. No meaningful attempt to find the treasure hidden beneath the hearth of our own home can evade this task, any more than those who feel drawn to Buddhism can escape reflective consideration of the Buddha. So it is to the figure of Christ that we now turn.

Chapter 2

From Jesus to Christ

Introduction

Not long ago, the residents' association to which I belong organised a visit to our local mosque, whose minaret I can see from my study window. We were greeted warmly and given a magnificent tea at the end of our visit. Between our arrival and the tea, we were ushered into the mosque's two immense prayer rooms, the upper one allowing us to see up to the great dome, with its fine Arabic lettering round the rim. The imam who spoke to us was Pakistani-born, but spoke fluent English, and addressed us directly and with humour. As he spoke about Muslim belief and practice, I felt just as the rich man must have felt when addressed by Abraham in Jesus' parable of Dives and Lazarus[1]: "Between us and you there is a great gulf fixed: so that they which would pass from hence to you cannot: neither can they pass to us, that would come from thence." (I quote from the Authorised Version, which is how it came to me.) In terms of belief, we inhabited different worlds. It was as if there was a thick plate-glass screen between us. And I thought, that is how it must feel to the average secular-minded person when listening to a Christian talking about their belief. "I believe that Jesus Christ is the Son of God, that he was born of a virgin, that he died to save us from our sins, and that he rose again from the dead."

Born and raised in this faith, participating in its rituals, breathing its atmosphere, I was – still am – as at home within it as the imam was in his faith. But certainly part of my motivation in leaving the priesthood was a glimmering awareness of this gulf, and a desire to reach across it: not to convert, but to create a bridge of understanding. Over the years since then, ensconced in the secular world and no longer in the formal structures of the

24

Church, I have become more and more conscious of the gulf. Robert Winston, in his book *The Story of God* [2], describes his experience in terms of a struggle with God, a lifelong attempt to resolve the conflict "as an averagely rational scientist and as a Jew."

Looking across the gulf, the first thing we need to do is to acknowledge that Jesus was not a Christian; like Robert Winston, he was a Jew. So some idea of how he fits into first-century Judaism might be a good place to start, and the greatest expert in this field is the (now late) first Professor of Jewish Studies at Oxford, Geza Vermes. Born in Hungary of Jewish parents in 1924, he was baptized out of concern for his safety, and became a Roman Catholic priest in an order devoted to biblical scholarship. After the war he renounced – or perhaps rather emerged from – his Catholic faith, wishing to return to his Jewish roots, He married, adopted British citizenship, and became the leading British scholar to work on the Dead Sea Scrolls, to which reference will be made later. According to Vermes, Jesus fits into a pattern of first-century "charismatic" Judaism – that is to say not that of the formal "establishment" but of the informal, inspirational, prophetic individuals whose authority was self-authenticating, and to whom people turned for healing of their ills and exorcism of their demons. "The religion proclaimed by Jesus was a wholly theocentric (God-centred) one in which he played the role of the man of God par excellence, the prophet of prophets, the shepherd of the flock, the leader, revealer and teacher without being himself in any sense the object of worship as he later became in the fully fledged Christianity created by Paul and John, and especially from the second century onwards."[3]

"The Good Man Jesus and the Scoundrel Christ"
Philip Pullman's provocative title has, of course, provoked outrage among many Christians. Nonetheless it should remind anyone beginning the task of "digging beneath his own hearth"

to recognise at the outset that there is a distinction – drawn, as we have already seen, by Geza Vermes – between the figure that emerges from the pages of the gospels and the figure who was transformed (mainly by St. Paul, in Pullman's view) into "the scoundrel Christ". This is how Pullman puts it. "There was the man Jesus, whom the gospels talked about, and there was the other sort of being, Christ, the Messiah, who featured more prominently in the Epistles. In the letters Paul wrote, he used the term 'Christ' 150 or so times, and 'Jesus' about 30. Paul is clearly much more interested in Christ; by the time he wrote, a generation or so after the crucifixion, the myth was already overtaking the man."[4]

The "mythologising" of great religious teachers is by no means confined to Christianity. The Jewish scriptures which were so influential in forming the imagination of Jesus show this process at work in regard to Moses, Elijah and others. In the sixth century BCE the Indian prince Gautama became to his disciples the Buddha, or "The Enlightened One;" and in the seventh century CE the Arabian merchant Kothan, whose profound experiences in the cave outside Mecca are enshrined in the Quran, became to his people Muhammad, "The Praised One." We can gratefully recognise that the Buddha and Moses, Christ and Muhammad, belong first and foremost to the human race rather than only to the particular religions which have issued from them. Anyone – Jew, Muslim, Christian or atheist – can accept that the profound discoveries the Buddha made about human existence and passed on in the Four Noble Truths, as well as the practical framework for living contained in the Noble Eightfold Path, are not just for Buddhists but for all human beings. No less true is it the case with the one whom his earliest followers came to call "The Anointed One", the Christ; indeed, it will be suggested that the "Lord's Prayer" can be used by anyone, religious or not, as a focus for their own reflection.

"Christ," Jung wrote, "lived a concrete, personal and unique life, which in all its essential features had at the same time an archetypal character. This character can be recognised from the numerous connections of the biographical details with world-wide myth-motifs… In the gospels themselves factual reports, legends and myths are woven into a whole. This is precisely what constitutes the meaning of the gospels."[5] It is held by most scholars that this weaving of fact and myth had already begun some time before St. Paul put pen to paper in about 50 CE, that is to say twenty years or so after Jesus' death and about twenty years before the first gospel, Mark, came to be written. From the beginning, then, shortly after the crucifixion, the historical Jesus activated "primordial images" or "archetypes" within the imaginations of those who henceforth began to refer to him as "The Anointed One" (in Greek "Christ"), or "The Saviour" or "The Lord". The skill that has to be developed, then, is the skill of the child of a mixed marriage, at home in the languages both of her mother and her father. For the fundamentalist the distinction between the two languages does not exist; walking on water, raising the dead, feeding multitudes are seen as fact, not myth. Any attempt, however, to engage with Christianity as a possible resource for contemporary living needs to bear the distinction in mind and to have a rudimentary idea of how the gospels came to be written.

From Oral Tradition to Written Gospels

Scholars are agreed that none of the four gospels was written by eyewitnesses, and that the earliest, Mark, could not have been written before 65-70 CE. What went on in the forty-odd years after the crucifixion can only be conjectured, but it is generally agreed that it was a time when "Jesus stories" were circulated and handed on by word of mouth, by "oral tradition". Some idea of how this happened can be gained by a comparison with John Steinbeck's affectionate memoir of his friend Ed Ricketts, prototype for "Doc" in *Cannery Row* and other books. When news reached Ricketts' friends that a train had smashed into his old car on a railroad crossing near New Monterey (he died two days' later), they instinctively clung together to talk about him, to exchange reminiscences and stories which conveyed the effect he had had on them. "Maybe some of the events are imagined. And perhaps some very small happenings may have grown out of all proportion in the mind. But no-one who knew him will deny the force and influence of Ed Ricketts. Everyone near him was influenced by him, deeply and permanently."[6]

During the first 30 years after the crucifixion those who had been influenced by Jesus "deeply and permanently" must have told their stories again and again. It is these stories, told and retold and perhaps assuming different shapes in the different places to which they percolated in the course of time, which form the basis of the first written traditions. The spur for writing them down was probably, first, the deaths of the original eyewitnesses and, second, the spread of the "Jesus movement" far beyond its original home into places far from that home and from one another – and dominated by a very different culture. Much the same process can be seen at work in Buddhism, only in its case the period of oral tradition was a good deal longer, something over five hundred years. The fact that it was only then that the Buddhist scriptures came to be written down was because, in the words of the great Buddhist scholar Edward Conze, "at that time the decline in faith threatened their continued survival in the memories of the monks. Different schools wrote down different things. Much of it was obviously composed centuries ago, and some of it must represent the direct and actual sayings of the Buddha himself."[7] In spite of the fact that like the Buddha himself Jesus left no actual written record of his teaching, New Testament scholars are agreed that while some at least of the sayings ascribed to him in the gospels were almost certainly *not* spoken by him, there are good grounds for accepting that much of the material in the gospels *does* represent the direct and actual sayings of Jesus himself.

One way to begin to appreciate the "double-decker" nature of the gospels – their mixture of biography and myth – might be to undertake a little simple detective work to see how traditions which probably have a common source got altered as they were handed down, perhaps in different versions or collections; in the process, that is to say, of transmission. Two examples may be taken from the Gospel of Luke to illustrate the point. In the first we shall compare Luke and John; in the second, Luke and Mark.

Luke 5: 1-10

While the people pressed upon (Jesus) to hear the word of God, he was standing by the lake of Gennesaret. And he saw two boats by the lake, but the fishermen had gone out of them and were washing their nets. Getting into one of the boats, which was Simon's, he asked him to put out a little from the land. And he sat down and taught the people from the boat. And when he had ceased speaking, he said to Simon, "Put out into the deep and let down your nets for a catch." Simon answered, "Master, we toiled all night and took nothing! But at your word I will let down the nets." And when they had done this, they enclosed a great shoal of fish, and as their nets were breaking, they beckoned to their partners in the other boat to come and help them. And they came and filled both the boats, so that they began to sink. But when Simon Peter saw it, he fell down at Jesus' knees, saying, "Depart from me, for I am a sinful man, O Lord." For he was astonished, and all that were with him, at the catch of fish which they had taken; and so also were James and John, sons of Zebedee, who were partners with Simon. And Jesus said to Simon, "Do not be afraid; henceforth you will be catching men."

John 21: 1-8

After this Jesus revealed himself again to the disciples by the

Sea of Tiberias; and he revealed himself in this way. Simon Peter, Thomas called the Twin, Nathanael of Cana in Galilee, the sons of Zebedee, and two others of his disciples were together. Simon Peter said to them, "I am going fishing." They said to him, "We will go with you." They went out and got into the boat; but that night they caught nothing.

Just as day was breaking, Jesus stood on the beach; yet the disciples did not know that it was Jesus. Jesus said to them, "Children, have you any fish?" They answered him, "No." He said to them, "Cast the net on the right side of the boat, and you will find some." So they cast it, and now they were not able to haul it in, for the quantity of fish. That disciple whom Jesus loved said to Peter, "It is the Lord!" When Simon Peter heard that it was the Lord, he put on his clothes, for he was stripped for work, and sprang into the sea. But the other disciples came in the boat, dragging the net full of fish, for they were not far from land, but about a hundred yards off.

The similarities between the two stories are obvious. But while in Luke's version the setting is the start of Jesus' ministry, in John's it is recorded as a "resurrection appearance," i.e. three years' later. Now it is possible that the two authors were using a common, written source. We shall see examples of where this certainly happened; but in this case the differences are significant enough to make it more likely that the two writers were making use of a common original story (oral, at least at first) handed down in different forms in two independent traditions, and moulding it, each in his particular way, to fit into and illustrate the story he wanted to tell. These two passages also reveal something of the two levels on which the gospels have to be read, corresponding to Jung's "biographical details" and "myth-motifs." Both have a kind of supernatural, "mythical" air about them, and in both Jesus is referred to as "the Lord," a title which was not used until after his death. On the other hand, both probably go back to an original "fishing event" in which Peter was involved. Our second pair of stories also illustrates the possibility that the authors had before them two versions of what was originally a single story.

Luke 7: 36-39
One of the Pharisees (named in verse 40 as Simon) asked Jesus to eat with him, and he went into the Pharisee's house, and sat at table. And behold, a woman of the city, who was a sinner, when she learned that he was sitting at table in the Pharisee's house, brought an alabaster flask of ointment, and standing behind him at his feet, weeping, she began to wet his feet with her tears, and wiped them with the hair of her head, and kissed his feet, and anointed them with the ointment. Now when the Pharisee who had invited him saw it, he said to himself, "If this man were a prophet, he would have known who and what sort of woman this is who is touching him, for she is a sinner." (Jesus then proceeds to reprove the critical Pharisee, and ends by saying to the woman: "Your faith has saved you; go in peace.")

Mark14: 3-5
And while (Jesus) was at Bethany in the house of Simon the leper, as he sat at table, a woman came with an alabaster jar of ointment, very costly, and she broke the jar and poured it over his head. But there were some who said to themselves indignantly, "Why was the ointment wasted? For this ointment might have been sold for more than three hundred denarii, and given to the poor."

Again, the similarities between the two stories are obvious: Jesus sitting at table in the house of one Simon; the woman with the alabaster box of ointment, the criticism and Jesus' justification of the woman's action; but the differences are significant (was the "original" Simon a Pharisee, or was he a leper?). Here again the differences make it likely that the authors received their story in two independent traditions, giving them a slant (to which, of course, they themselves may have added) appropriate to the particular place to which they have assigned them in the composition of their gospels; Luke, for example, places the story near the beginning of Jesus' ministry, while Mark places it right at the end as a prelude to the Last Supper. It may be, too, that these differences were dictated by the circumstances of the audience the author was addressing.

The Gospels and the Christian Community

If the gospel writers made use of stories handed down in one form in one place, and in another form in another, there is also evidence that two of them – Matthew and Luke – used a common written source, or rather two common written sources. The first source was Mark, nearly all of whose gospel appears word for word in the first and third gospels. A quick reading of Mark 2: 1-7, Luke 5: 17-31, and Matthew 9: 1-12 makes this obvious. There are various technical reasons why scholars are almost unanimously agreed that Mark's was the original, rather than one of the other two, and no more need be said about this. Unlike Mark, the second source does not exist as an independent document. Known by scholars as "Q", its existence is deduced from those non-Marcan passages which Matthew and Luke have in common and which are frequently identical in wording. Perhaps a written collection of "Jesus sayings" was made at some stage towards the end of the oral tradition period. Perhaps there were other such written collections; maybe Mark himself had access to one or more such collections when he came to write his gospel. At any rate, the Parable of the Lost Sheep, found only in Matthew and Luke, obviously comes from a common written source (Luke 15: 1 – 7, Matthew18: 1 – 4 and 10 – 14). But why the differences in context between the two gospels' versions? In Luke's version the story is told to the scribes and Pharisees, in the context of their complaints about Jesus mixing with sinners. In Matthew's version it is told to the disciples, in the context of their question about greatness in the kingdom of heaven. We have seen how Luke and John gave different contexts to the fishing story, and how Luke and Mark did the same thing with the anointing story. In the case of the parable of the Lost Sheep, which audience, and which context and message, is likely to be original? Perhaps neither. Scholars have been generally agreed since the 1920s that the "ingredients" used by the gospel writers came to them in most cases without context, and that it is the author who has supplied it. Here, in addition to the audience being different, the application of the parable is also different.

Why does all this matter? To put it shortly, because we cannot with integrity be two people at the same time – accepting the scientific method in every area save one. No spirituality can be worthwhile which requires us to step out of the culture to which we belong. A contemporary spirituality must be a critical spirituality, and a spirituality whose focus is Christ has to include some awareness of the context of his life and teaching, and of the ways in which they have been transmitted. This means throwing out the idea that the gospels are simple biographies of Jesus, even though we can be sure that they contain some – very brief – biographical details. Each gospel is the product of an author using the materials that he had to hand, most of which have the feel of going back to original oral reminiscences, however much they may have developed during transmission. With these materials he fashioned a work which both expressed his own convictions and also was directed to particular people in particular circumstances. In the case of the parable of The Lost Sheep, Luke seems to have used it to illustrate a recurring theme in his gospel, the contrast between the welcome given to Jesus by the sinners, the outcast and despised, and the hostility of the "establishment". Matthew, on the other hand, has used it to convey a message to what had by his time become "the Church", exhorting its members to care for the younger or more fragile among them.

Two particular circumstances are worth mentioning. The first has to do with the dilemma facing the Christian community once it began to move out of its Jewish homeland. Was it to continue as a Jewish sect, or could non-Jews become part of it without becoming Jews first? The issue appears to have caused as much of a rumpus as the issue of homosexuality in the contemporary church; an account of it can be read in Paul's letter to the Galatians, chapter two. Paul (Pullman's villain), ex-Pharisee and now impassioned Christian convert, championed the "liberal tendency" and had to defend himself against the charge of being an upstart, since unlike Peter he had not been a member of Jesus' original band of disciples. We have two accounts of the meeting that was held to discuss the issue, for as well as Paul's account there is a much toned-down account, written a good deal later, in chapter 15 of Acts. Paul's version has a much more realistic ring about it, hot with the passion that we are used to seeing in religious disputes. "When Cephas (Peter) came to Antioch I opposed him to his face... I said to (him) before them all, 'If you, though a Jew, live like a Gentile, and not like a Jew, how can you compel the Gentiles to live like Jews?'"[8] Peter, like some modern bishop anxious not to upset his fundamentalist constituents, had plainly back-tracked from the liberal position he had, perhaps reluctantly, arrived at in regard to Gentile converts. But for Paul there could be no fudging the issue. The Church had to recognise that it had entered into a new era, in which the stipulations about circumcision and food laws laid down in the Bible no longer applied. This is a lesson the contemporary Church still needs to learn, that new eras involve being prepared to jettison some things previous eras regarded as essential. In the end Paul won the day, and Luke's gospel reflects the liberal position which by the time he wrote his gospel, some forty years' later, had become well established.

The second circumstance was the consequence of the first. As a result of the Christian community's eventual decision to allow Gentiles to dispense with Jewish food laws and the rite of circumcision, it was formally excommunicated from the Jewish fold. Bitterness will have been felt on both sides, as well as within the Christian movement itself, between the fundamentalists, still insisting on circumcision, and the liberals. Matthew's and John's gospels both reveal the scars of this bitterness, and the anti-Semitic prejudice for which they have given an excuse is a matter of the utmost shame. While Jesus certainly did, like Jeremiah before him, condemn what he regarded as the distortions of Judaism for which he felt that some of the religious authorities were responsible, he lived and died as a Jew, and chose none but Jews as his disciples. If, however, he restricted his own activity to the Jewish homeland and among his fellow Jews, there is evidence that this did not preclude him from reaching out to non-Jews: the Samaritan woman in John, the Syrophoenician woman in Mark and the centurion in Luke.[9] There may or may not have been more such instances, but his later followers who included them in their reminiscences seem to have felt that they gave good grounds for claiming, as Paul put it, that he "has made us (i.e. Jews and non-Jews) one, and has broken down the dividing wall of hostility."[10]

The Gospels and the Old Testament

Steinbeck's observation that in the passing on (the "tradition") of stories about Ed Ricketts some of the events may have been imagined and that some small happenings may have grown out of all proportion in the mind tells us that the human capacity for myth-making is just as potent in the present era as in that long past. It is particularly likely to happen in the case of such larger-than-life characters as Winston Churchill or Martin Luther King, who came to exercise a strong hold on people's imaginations, and to express for them their hopes and aspirations. It is this same tendency that can be observed in the Jesus tradition. We are not left with a stark choice between the fundamentalist's naïveté and the reductionist's dismissal (both are literalists), but have to bear in mind continually the "double-decker" nature of the gospels, their inseparable mixture of Jung's "biographical details and myth-motifs". Exactly the same mixture is observable in the scriptures of Buddhism, where, as Joseph Campbell remarks, "the biography of Gautama was turned into a supernatural life through a constellation of many of the same motifs. Through such a process history is lost; but history also is made. For the function of such myth-making is *to interpret the sense, not to chronicle the facts, of a life,* and to offer the artwork of the legend, then, as an activating symbol for the inspiration and shaping of lives, and even civilisations, to come"[11] (italics mine). Some wise words of Martin Buber are as appropriate to the study of Jesus as they are to the study of Moses for which they were written. "We must adopt a critical approach and seek reality... by asking ourselves what human relation to real events this could have been which led gradually, along many bypaths and by way of many metamorphoses, from mouth to ear, from one memory to another, and from dream to dream, until it grew into the written account we have read."[12]

The title of this chapter, "From Jesus to Christ," gives an indication of the crucial development resulting from the impact made by Jesus on his earliest followers, a development similar to that which we have seen in the ascription of the titles Buddha and Muhammad. If Jung's concept of archetypes is accepted, we could say that their encounter with Jesus had awakened his disciples to the "God-image" within them. This may seem theoretical and obscure, but something written by the American psychologist Abraham Maslow might give a clue to what is meant. "Every human being (he wrote) has (two) sets of forces within him. One set clings to safety and defensiveness out of fear, tending to regress backward, hanging on to the past..., afraid to take chances, afraid to jeopardize what he already has, afraid of independence, freedom and separateness. The other set of forces impels him forward toward wholeness of self and uniqueness of self, toward full functioning of all his capacities, toward confidence in the face of the external world."[13] If the function of the "God-image" is to represent this wholeness of self, it seems that the function of the Christ-archetype is to present a model of complete responsiveness to this God-image. The person poised, as all are, between Maslow's two sets of forces is beckoned forward by the Christ archetype, away from fear and defensiveness towards the full functioning of all her or his capacities. This might help to explain the astonishing access of energy those earliest followers of Jesus experienced after his death and which, we will suggest, led to the resurrection narratives. All four gospels contain stories of blind men being given their sight, and it may be that the significance of these stories was seen to lie in the experience of those men and women: "One thing I know, that though I was blind, now I see."[14] If the scribes and Pharisees, who appear in the gospels as more or less "cartoon" characters, give archetypal expression to the forces of defensiveness and fear, then – it being, as we have seen Joseph Campbell putting it, the function of mythology to supply the symbols that carry the human spirit forward – the ascription of the title Christ to Jesus expresses their conviction that he had enabled them to move towards that "wholeness of self" for which the code word in the New Testament is "salvation".

The process by which Jesus became Christ naturally played an important part in shaping the gospels, both during the earliest stage of the oral tradition and when it came to be written down. In other words, as the biographical details – the real events – were transmitted "from mouth to ear, from one memory to another," they will have been coloured by their relation to the "myth-motifs" resident in the imaginations of those who so transmitted them. Dream must be reckoned with, as well as mouth, ear, and memory. We may put it starkly by saying that alongside the biographical memories, the oral and written traditions which make up the source material of the gospels, must be included in the influence (the "flowing-in") of the Old Testament. This, after all, was the repository of the myths which defined the culture to which Jesus and his earliest followers belonged.

"One fact is certain," writes Vermes: "the identification of Jesus, not just with *a* Messiah, but with *the* awaited Messiah of Judaism, belonged to the heart and kernel of the earliest phase of Christian belief."[15] The key figure for the "Messiah archetype" in the minds of Jews in the first century was David, and it is not hard to see why. To all outward appearances the Jews were an insignificant people, again and again in the course of their history defeated, exiled, their land occupied by an alien power. Assyria, Babylon, the empires of Alexander, Egypt, Syria, and most recently Rome – it was with these that power and influence lay. But David, while he personified their hopes that one day their kingdom would recover the greatness it had enjoyed for so brief a time under his rule, also symbolised another conviction. Of the sons of Jesse, David was the youngest; in the eyes of his father, his brothers, and even the great prophet Samuel, the one least likely to be a candidate for kingship. Yet it was he who was chosen, for "the LORD sees not as man sees; man looks on the outward appearance, but the LORD looks on the heart."[16] And it was he and not the mighty men of valour who with a sling and a stone slew the great adversary Goliath.[17] Truly, as the Jewish people sang in one of what they knew as the "Psalms of David," "the stone which the builders rejected has become the head of the corner."[18] (This was a text, incidentally, which Christians were in their turn to apply to Jesus.[19]) So as well as nourishing a nationalist hope of future political greatness the figure of David also nourished, or at least admitted of, a conviction that God would use their very insignificance as the means by which one day his kingdom would be established.

What is usually called conversion seems to have taken the form, in those early followers, of a sudden or gradual awareness which, so to speak, lit the touch paper to the fuse provided by the Jewish scriptures and first-century Jewish expectation. As they reflected on the decisive shift that had occurred in them, and continued their inner dialogue with the myths and legends in which since birth they had been immersed, more and more each seemed to illuminate the other. Of central importance, naturally, was the death of Jesus, the shocking event which at first seemed to fly in the face of every image of a victorious Messiah. But in the light of their experience their minds ranged the scriptures again; and from their pages there emerged a pattern – we could say an archetype – for the kind of Messiah, or "Christ" (the Greek translation), they believed Jesus to be. Their reflections seem particularly to have turned to Psalm 22. It contains 31 verses, and like a number of other psalms it starts (verses 1-21) with a cry of anguish and a recounting of bitter affliction:

Psalm 22:1-21 (abridged)
My God, my God, why hast thou forsaken me?

Why art thou so far from helping me, from the words of my groaning?

All who see me mock at me, they make mouths at me, they wag their heads;

"He committed his cause to the Lord; let him deliver him, let him rescue him, for he delights in him!"

My strength is dried up like a potsherd,

And my tongue cleaves to my jaws;

Thou dost lay me in the dust of death.

A company of evildoers encircle me;

They have pierced my hands and my feet –

I can count all my bones –

They stare and gloat over me;

They divide my garments among them,
And for my raiment they cast lots.

A reading of Mark's account of the crucifixion (Mark 15: 21-39) at once reveals echoes of these words. But then, at verse 22, the mood of the psalm changes dramatically. Desolation is turned into vindication, tears into joy:

Psalm 22: 22-31 (abridged)
I will tell of thy name to my brethren,
In the midst of the congregation I will praise thee;
All you sons of Jacob, glorify him,
And stand in awe of him, all you sons of Israel!
For he has not despised or abhorred
The affliction of the afflicted;
And he has not hid his face from him.
All the ends of the earth shall remember
And turn to the LORD;
And all the families of the nations
Shall worship before him.
Men shall tell of the Lord to the coming generation,
And proclaim his deliverance to a people yet unborn.

If the earlier section of the psalm resonated with their reflections on the death of Jesus, these later verses must have resonated with what they described as their experience of Jesus "risen", and of the energy which they felt impelling them to carry what by now they were describing as the gospel ("good news") beyond the Jewish homeland to "all the families of the nations".

Previous generations of readers (and fundamentalists still) saw in Psalm 22 a remarkable prophecy of the Passion. We can now see, however, that the current flows the other way; that the reflections of the earliest Christians on Psalm 22 actually entered into their telling of the story of the suffering and death of Jesus and of his subsequent vindication (for however the Resurrection is understood this, for them, was its significance). So we can now add to our list of sources of the gospels, if not a (written?) collection of "proof-texts", at least some kind of cumulative process by which allusions or even actual words from the Old Testament became fused with the traditions. One final pair of passages will serve as an example.

Luke 7: 11-17

Soon afterward (Jesus) went to a city called Nain, and his disciples and a great crowd with him. As he drew near to the gate of the city, behold, a man who had died was being carried out, the only son of his mother, and she was a widow; and a large crowd from the city was with her. And when the Lord saw her, he had compassion on her and said to her, "Do not weep." And he came and touched the bier, and the bearers stood still. And he said, "Young man, I say to you, arise." And the dead man sat up, and began to speak. And he gave him to his mother. Fear seized them all; and they glorified God, saying, "A great prophet has arisen among us!" and "God has visited his people."

1 Kings 17: 17-24 (abridged)

After this the son of a widow became ill; and his illness was so severe that there was no breath left in him. And (Elijah) carried him up into the upper chamber, where he lodged, and laid him upon his own bed. Then he stretched himself upon the child three times, and cried to the LORD, "O LORD my God, let this child's soul come into him again." And the LORD hearkened to the voice of Elijah; and the soul of the child came into him again, and he revived. And Elijah took the child, and delivered him to his mother. And the woman said to Elijah, "Now I know that you are a man of God, and that the word of the LORD in your mouth is truth."

The similarities are obvious. What probably happened was that in the course of transmission a Jesus story became attracted to an Elijah story, perhaps as it circulated in Galilee, the main focus Jesus' ministry, where according to Vermes there is likely to have existed "a lively local folk memory concerning the miraculous deeds of the great prophet Elijah."[20] Both David and Elijah were potent symbols in the imaginations of Jews of the period, symbols which Jesus touched and activated so that, having lain dormant, they were roused to life in such a way that their lives took on a new direction.

Before leaving the subject of the Old Testament's influence on the gospels we must turn, finally, to the most influential figure of all in Jewish imagination, both then and now: Moses. The Jewish celebration of Passover every year is a reminder of why Moses occupies such an important place in Jewish imagination, reinforced century after century as members of this ancient people cried out from dispossession, defeat, pogroms, ghettoes, death camps. Moses stood for deliverance, he who in that archetypical act of deliverance had under the hand of God rescued his people from slavery in Egypt and brought them across the Red Sea to their own land. But he was more than a figure from the past, for in his lips they had placed a promise: "The LORD your God will raise up for you a prophet like me from among you, from your brethren – him you shall heed."[21] The men and women caught up in the Jesus movement in its earliest days made sense of the impact he had made upon them by fitting onto him images from their culturally-conditioned imaginations, so it is hardly surprising that in addition to those for whom he seemed to fit the David or Elijah archetype, there were many for whom he was none other than the promised Moses, raised up from among them. Of course as the Jesus movement grew out of its Jewish homeland and spread into Gentile cultures, these Jewish archetypes became less relevant, but we can still see something of the early Christians' fascination with them in the birth stories narrated by Matthew and Luke. Matthew's account of the massacre of the children by Herod, and the rescue of Jesus[22], clearly echoes the Exodus story of the birth and rescue of Moses, and of Pharaoh's order that every son born to the Hebrews was to be cast into the Nile.[23] Luke's birth story, by contrast, belongs to the David-Messiah tradition. Against all historical probability, Jesus is brought from Nazareth to Bethlehem, "royal David's city," to be born in fulfilment of the promise that "the Lord God will give to him the throne of his father David"[24]; and it is shepherds, evocative of the shepherd boy David, who are the first to greet him, rather than Matthew's "wise men from the east." Both stories, in other words, are mythological, and attempts to reconcile them or "historicize" them are utterly misguided.

How do we see Jesus?

As head of a Religious Education department, I believed that it was important that every pupil should have some knowledge of the basic story of Jesus as outlined in the gospels. It formed, therefore, a major part of the curriculum in pupils' last two years, before leaving or going into the Sixth Form. What I came to learn after some time was that it was necessary to confront them with their preconceived opinions – opinions which by and large they had picked up from their parents or other adults. So I decided to get them to submit Jesus to an aggression test. This was based on a test which formed part of a unit on social issues – in this case violence. An excellent course book on the subject included the test, whose object was to demonstrate that aggression was a necessary part of everyone's make-up, minimal in some, pronounced in others. There were twenty questions, with three possible responses to each; for example, you are in a café, and someone coming in treads on your foot and apologises. Do you say: (a) Sorry, it was my fault; (b) Can't you watch where you're going? (c) That's OK – forget it. Once the twenty questions had been completed, they were scored; 1 for the least aggressive, in this case (a), 2 for the average (c), 3 for the most aggressive (b). Those who were willing to share their scores with the class at the end demonstrated clearly the difference in their personalities. The maximum score, of course, was 60, which thankfully none of my pupils recorded! The deviser of the test suggested that a healthy score would be, as far as I remember, between 35 and 45.

Using this model, I devised twenty questions to test Jesus, in each case using a genuine response from the gospels, slightly disguised, and adding two other imaginary, but possible, ones. For example: Peter severely criticises Jesus for warning him of his impending suffering. Does Jesus then say to Peter: (a) What you have said is true, I will choose a different course; (b) Shut up, devil; (c) Thanks for your concern, but you are wrong. Without exception, in the many classes to whom I gave this test over the years, the scores recorded by my pupils put Jesus below the 30 mark, and they were astonished when I told them that in fact he had scored (again, as far as I remember) 45. This demonstrated to me beyond doubt that the model of Jesus lodged in the imaginations of the great majority of people was totally inadequate as a paradigm, or "ego-ideal", for robust adulthood.

How did Jesus see himself?

We have seen something of the way in which the early followers of Jesus understood him. Whether or not these archetypal connexions were made by Jesus himself, his early followers certainly ascribed to him the new understanding they felt they had gained of their scriptures. "He opened their minds to understand the scriptures;"[25] and "beginning with Moses and the prophets, he interpreted to them in all the scriptures the things concerning himself."[26] At any rate, according to the almost unanimous opinion of scholars it is extremely unlikely that Jesus ever applied the title "Messiah" to himself, and where the gospels say that he did we should ascribe it rather to a process of "reading back" into the lifetime of Jesus an apprehension of him at which Christians arrived only later, and as we have seen almost certainly before the appearance of Paul. (In Pullman's retelling of the gospel story, this was the role Jesus' twin brother Christ wanted to foist upon him, and Jesus fervently rejected.)

Is there any evidence of how Jesus did see himself, and the role he felt called to fulfil? The ascription that appears to answer this question most closely is "God's servant." The term is a favourite one of the author (or authors) of the last third of the Old Testament book of Isaiah. There it appears to be used of an individual, as in the famous chapter 53 describing the "man of sorrows and acquainted with grief;" but elsewhere it is plain that the term is used for the Jewish people as a whole, in the writer's time (he is referred to by scholars as "Second" Isaiah) nearing the end of their period of suffering and exile at the hand of Babylon. So the servant also stands, in the words of the author, for "Israel whom I have chosen."[27] The same characteristic of an individual representing a people appears in the Psalms – Psalm 22 has already been quoted at length. Poetry has a way of entering the subconscious, and this colourful collection of Jewish poetry, along with the great myths of his people to which Jesus was doubtless exposed since birth, must also have helped to shape his imagination. It is these, in Theodore Roszak's phrase, that will have given to the mind of Jesus images to think with.

Of crucial importance in the development of his self-understanding was undoubtedly his baptism by John the Baptist, at (according to the gospels) around the age of 30. Here the terms "servant" and "son" meet – in Greek, the language in which the gospels were written, the same word is used for both. The words in which Jesus' baptism experience is recorded, "Thou art my beloved Son, in thee I am well pleased,"[28] recall similar words from that part of Isaiah referred to above: "Behold my servant…, my chosen, in whom my soul delights; I have put my spirit upon him."[29] Here, by the river Jordan, was the experience which profoundly changed his life, setting it on the course which was to lead ultimately to his death. As the Buddha's experience under the bodhi or pipal tree in the Buddhist tradition and Muhammad's experience in the cave in the Muslim tradition mark the beginning of the great movements with which they are associated, so in the original telling of the Christian story it is with Jesus' baptism, rather than with his birth, that the gospel begins.

If Jesus saw himself as God's servant, then, he interpreted it in terms of sonship. Although it is generally agreed that John's gospel was the last to be written, it is here that the "son-father" relationship is most emphasised. The words "Father" or "My Father" occur about a hundred times in that gospel, four times as often as in the other three gospels put together. And no saying in that gospel expresses with greater clarity Jesus' consciousness of the subservience of his ego to a greater Self than the words the author puts into his mouth: "I seek not my own will but the will of him (the Father) who sent me."[30] Interestingly enough the mythical account of the "Temptations (or more properly "Testings") in the Wilderness", handed down in the "Q" tradition by Matthew and Luke as a sequel to the Baptism story, also picture him working out his mission in terms of the relationship of Son to Father; just as, following Mark, they put into his mouth the words "Father, not what I will, but what thou wilt"[31] in their account of Jesus' prayer in the Garden of Gethsemane.

There is another title used enigmatically by Jesus for himself which appears frequently in the gospels, but then seems to have completely disappeared in Christian usage: Son of Man. Huge amounts have been written about this (to us) curious way for anyone to talk about himself, but again it has to be seen in the context of Jewish mythology, for certainly one of its associations is with the mysterious figure of the Son of Man in the Book of Daniel. In that book he represents the faithful Jews suffering under the tyranny of a hated ruler in the second century BCE.

The passage assures them that they will be vindicated and that despite their present humiliations theirs, too, is the promise given to this "one like a son of man," namely "dominion and glory and kingdom, that all peoples, nations, and languages should serve him; his dominion is an everlasting dominion, which shall not pass away, and his kingdom one which shall not be destroyed."[32] It is easy to understand how the image of vindication following humiliation will have acted as an anchor to the imagination of Jesus as he faced opposition and humiliation at the hands of the religious authorities.

This brings us to the subject of the "kingdom of God", a term frequently found on the lips of Jesus in the gospels, and one which the first three agree was the central subject of his preaching. However elusive the concept is to us, it was intensely real to first-century Jews; indeed it can be said to have dominated their imagination. Israel's task, after all, was to prepare for the coming of the kingdom of God, and the Essenes of Qumran, that strange community which has left us the Dead Sea Scrolls and which was more or less contemporary with Jesus, went out into the desert deliberately to prepare for the imminently expected coming of the kingdom.

What did Jesus understand by the kingdom? No simple answer can be given, for it seems to have been a term which for him incorporated several different aspects. Certainly his opening proclamation, "The time is fulfilled, and the kingdom of God is at hand,"[33] expressed his conviction that something urgent, new and thrilling, is about to happen; not only about to happen, but in some sense had already started happening. Asked by the Pharisees when the kingdom of God was coming, Jesus replied, according to Luke, "The kingdom of God is in the midst of you."[34] Many-faceted as his understanding of the kingdom of God appears to have been, it was undoubtedly a living archetype for Jesus. It was for him a new reality, indifferent to the status of saint and sinner, Jew and Gentile, which in one sense he personally embodied and in another sense it was his vocation to usher in. "He thought," writes E.P. Sanders, "that God was about to bring in his kingdom, and that he, Jesus, was God's last emissary. He thought therefore that he was in some sense 'king'. He rode into Jerusalem on an ass, recalling a prophecy about the king riding on an ass, and he was executed for claiming to be 'king of the Jews'." Nevertheless, Sanders goes on, "Jesus seems to have been quite reluctant to adopt a title for himself. I think that even 'king' is not precisely correct, since Jesus regarded God as king. My own favourite term for his conception of himself is 'viceroy.' God was king, but Jesus represented him and would represent him in the coming kingdom."[35]

For us today of course the kingdom of God cannot carry the same rich resonances that it carried for first-century Jews. In fact, by the time John's gospel came to be written, some time after the other three, the term seems to have disappeared almost completely. It is used only in two verses in chapter three, elsewhere being replaced by "life" or "eternal life", as in the words John ascribes to Jesus, "I came that they may have life, and have it abundantly."[36] It is certainly one, I think, which corresponds more nearly with an inchoate longing felt in some way by very many people, and connected by Teilhard with that restlessness which comes upon us in high streets and out-of-town stores. "What looks like no more than a hunger for material well-being is in reality a hunger for higher being."[37] Nevertheless, Jesus taught his disciples to pray for the coming of the kingdom, and we shall have occasion to return to the subject when we come to look at the Lord's Prayer.

Although some reference will be made to Paul's letters, no systematic attempt will be made to examine the truth of Philip Pullman's claim that it was Paul who turned "the good man Jesus" into "the scoundrel Christ". Having traced briefly the development of the oral tradition in which the historical figure of the man Jesus became the Messiah (or Christ) and an "object of devotion", we now need to have a closer look at his person and his teaching and their relation to contemporary culture.

Chapter 3

The Teaching of Jesus

This sudden plunge into textual analysis of the gospels may seem a far cry from the search for a meaningful spirituality. However, the reason for having at least a basic understanding of the nature and composition of the gospels is to ensure that whatever form this spirituality takes, it should not be cut off from that contemporary experience of ourselves and of our world to which the scientific method has contributed so much. At the same time, it is worth pondering an observation by Karen Armstrong in her magisterial survey of religion, *The Case for God*, about the reason the monks of mediaeval Europe devoted themselves to the reading of scripture. It was not "simply to acquire information but was a spiritual exercise that enabled them to enter their inner world and there confront the truths revealed in scripture to see how they measured up. Reading – in private or in the communal practice of the liturgy – was *part of the process of personal transformation.*"[1]

The objective of this book, it will be remembered, is to attempt to "dig beneath our own hearth" to see whether there is anything worthwhile to be found there; and if there is, whether it is of purely antique interest, or treasure which can contribute towards contemporary human living. We have discussed myth, the language of religion, and seen that it is distinct from (and complementary to) the language of science and historical fact. We have seen that within the gospels myth and historical fact are interwoven; that their writers were concerned not just to present to their readers narratives which they felt represented the character and teaching of their subject, but also the impact which he made upon his followers. For them, Jesus was "the Christ", fitting into and making sense of the mythology in which they had been brought up. The challenge with which the "Jesus movement" was confronted as soon as it moved out of its Jewish birthplace was (as it still is) how to do justice to the story of Jesus the Christ in terms of the new cultures into which it found itself moving.

Images of Wholeness

In a remarkable book, *The Jesus Sutras*,[2] Martin Palmer, Head of The Alliance of Religion and Conservation, writes about the discovery in northwestern China of a vast collection of scrolls which archaeological evidence indicates had been hidden in a cave walled up at the beginning of the eleventh century. Most of the scrolls were Buddhist, Confucian and Taoist, as would be expected. Alongside these scrolls, however, was another group: Christian scrolls, written in Chinese, telling the Christian story in terms of Chinese culture, and presenting a very different form of Christianity from that which became dominant in the West. Travelling along the ancient Silk Road, a Christian mission had arrived from Persia in about CE 635, and instead of imposing upon the people amongst whom they found themselves the forms and formalities of their own Christian practice, the Persian monks set about expressing their faith in terms of the very different culture of China. There was a precedent for this in the decisions made by the earliest Christian movement when it began to expand out of its original Jewish environment into a Gentile, or Greek, environment. The Chinese Christianity that grew out of the original Persian mission grew and flourished until it was virtually wiped out by persecution towards the end of the tenth century and the beginning of the eleventh. That seems to have been when the scrolls were walled up.

The story is fascinating in its own right, including the author's finding of an eighth-century pagoda looked after by a 115-year old Buddhist nun, who told him that local people knew that it had been founded by monks who had come from the West and had believed in One God – i.e. Christians. But the purpose of referring to it here is to underline the principle which it so clearly demonstrates, that if a spirituality is to be truly "owned" it must express itself in terms of the culture in which it finds itself. Writing more than 60 years ago, the English Dominican theologian Fr. Victor White recognised that already by that time "to many a modern man, the symbols employed by Christ and the Church have become every bit as obscure as the sarcophagus or titles of a Pharaoh. They leave him cold, because he no longer sees their significance and relevance to his own daily life. But (he went on) there are many who have rediscovered that significance and relevance through analytical psychology."[3] This does not, of course, imply signing up to a course of psychoanalysis, but it does imply a recognition of what has been learned in the last hundred years about human nature and its motivations. This, together with the dominance of the scientific outlook, has had a profound effect on Western culture, and made it as different from that of previous centuries as Gentile culture was from Jewish, or Chinese from Syrian.

Jung's theory of archetypes suggests that within the unconscious of human beings there exist "images of wholeness." He further suggests that if we use our imagination to cooperate with these images and allow them to work in our lives they will assist us in our growth towards wholeness (or "individuation" – becoming who you really are). The last chapter considered some of these images of wholeness in the unconscious of those first-century Jews whose imaginations were touched by Jesus. These images were not created by him; they were there already, given shape by the culture to which they belonged. Within the same cultural context it is understandable that in the imaginations of some Moses was the dominant figure, in others David, in others Elijah. But as we have seen, the spread of the Jesus movement beyond its original Jewish cradle must rapidly have made it apparent that talk of him in terms of these Jewish images simply failed to connect, in just the same way that "church-speak" fails to connect with the consciousness of most people under the age of forty in the culture of the West today. Those Jewish images failed not because there were no "images of wholeness" in the unconscious of non-Jews, but because in them the images were determined by a different culture, one for the most part in which the Hellenistic mystery religions exercised decisive influence. Originating in Greece, as their description implies, these had spread throughout the civilised world following the conquests of Alexander the Great three centuries' earlier. Taking many forms and often including the figure of a Saviour, they seem to have satisfied people's longing for "salvation"; by being initiated into the mysteries of whatever one of these Hellenistic religions the candidate felt touched by, she or he was given an orientation, a framework for their life. The great Jewish scholar Philo of Alexandria, a contemporary of Jesus, had already prepared the ground for what we can call Christianity's Gentile mission by explaining Judaism in terms which his far more numerous Greek-speaking and Greek-thinking fellow citizens might under-stand. Both Judaism and Christianity remained utterly distinct from the mystery religions, but with Philo a bridge had been built. So Jesus the Messiah became the Lord, the Saviour, the Son of God, as in seventh-century China he became the ultimate "Bodhisattva" in an authentic Chinese expression of Christianity which yet remained distinct from Buddhism.

The question now is whether further development is possible, appropriate to contemporary Western culture. It was a question pondered deeply by the German theologian Dietrich Bonhoeffer, executed at Flossenburg in Bavaria a month before the end of the Second World War. "If one day," he mused, "it becomes clear that the (religious) *a priori* does not exist at all, but was a historically conditioned and transient form of human self-expression, and if therefore man becomes radically religionless – and I think that this is already more or less the case… – what does that mean for

Christianity?"[4] Many would certainly reply that it meant its end, since in their view Christianity is irrevocably tied to a world view utterly alien to our own; it can therefore be of no more than historical or archaeological interest. But those who agree with Jung's contention that "it is not Christianity but our conception of it that has become antiquated" have to be prepared for disciplined, critical study of the gospels in the light of modern scientific scholarship, and for the kind of reflective assimilation that brings together the material read and our experience of ourselves. Both of these activities would seem to be essential in order that what Joseph Campbell calls "the vitalising image of the universal god-man who is actually immanent and effective in all of us may be somehow known to consciousness."[5]

False Self and True Self

In his important book *Experiment in Depth*, a study of the work of Jung, T.S.Eliot and Arnold Toynbee, P.W.Martin makes the following observation: "Christianity, more than any other faith perhaps, shows how great religious truths, now largely lost or traduced, may be recovered by direct experience of the other side of consciousness. In the Synoptic (i.e. the first three) Gospels, Jesus of Nazareth sets out in unmistakable terms the salient features of the individuation process, describing in detail both the dangers encountered and the means by which men and societies may become whole. The discoveries of analytical psychology do little else than repeat, in modern phraseology, and with detailed empirical backing, the principal injunctions of the Christian way."[6] Of primary importance in the teaching of Jesus, maintains Martin, "is separation from the *persona*. Those, such as the Scribes and Pharisees, who did everything for the sake of the external appearance, made clean the outside but paid no attention to the inside, are utterly condemned."[7] By the *persona* is meant the "face" we present to the world, the "mask" (the term comes from the mask worn by actors in Greek theatre) other people see: the doctor, the mechanic, the teacher, the housewife. Another term drawn from the theatre, "role", gets near to describing it. No one can avoid "playing a role" in some way; the danger is for us to become so identified with it that we neglect, or become ignorant of, the real person we are inside, which is plastic and malleable and cannot be confined within the narrow limits of the *persona*.

As Martin observes, the great religious truths of which Christianity was meant to be the guardian have been largely lost or traduced. Many of the most sensitive and concerned, not finding them there, have turned elsewhere – to Buddhism, for example, or Sufism – for inspiration. These great embodiments of religious truths from other cultures, fulfilling in those cultures that sense of "quest" identified by Robert Byron, may well be equally fulfilling to many in European and North American culture today. Many in this culture, however, may still hope to find within Christianity the great religious truths which Martin, like Jung, believed were to be found within it, and which need to be recovered. The critical, scientific study of the gospels on the one hand and the insights of analytical psychology on the other have made possible this recovery by presenting a new under-standing of the teaching of Jesus. The full import of this teaching, however, cannot be grasped without appreciating that it issues out of his own self-understanding.

It was suggested in the last chapter that Jesus understood himself in relation to God as Son to Father. How this self-under-standing began to dawn on him, we do not know, but the gospels make it clear that of decisive importance for him was his baptism by John the Baptist in the river Jordan. It is this event with which the earliest gospel, Mark, opens (there was nothing in the earliest traditions about his birth). The words expressing this full consciousness of his identity, "Thou art my beloved Son, with thee I am well pleased"[8], did not come to Jesus out of the blue but, as we have seen, from the book of Isaiah in which it is evident he was steeped. They do not necessarily imply uniqueness; indeed the last gospel to be written, John, suggests that "to all who received him, who believed in his name, he gave power to become children of God."[9] They do, however, imply a vivid awareness of the core of his being, an apprehension, (to employ the terms used by Martin) of his true Self, of his unconditional "loved-ness" and therefore of his "brotherness" in relation to every other human being. ("Self", with a capital, describes the true being of a person, as distinct from "self" without a capital, as used in the phrase "self-centredness".) The "voice" at Jesus' baptism was a living, convincing experience both of God and of humanity, the oneness of God and the oneness of humanity, monotheism and *monanthropism*. According to Mark, this is what gave authority to his teaching – "he taught with authority, and not as the scribes"[10]. People seem to have sensed that he was speaking from his true Self, not through a mask, for after all he had no mask, no role. He was not a scribe, he had no official religious position, but he did have that inner authority which no role can give and which evokes a response that no "authoritarian" preaching can ever do.

Jesus' apprehension of himself as "beloved son" is, as we have seen, reflected in his teaching, and represents the main thrust of those discourses which the traditions have preserved and which meet us in the pages of the gospels. Taking fully into account the alterations, shiftings of emphasis, additions even, dictated by the particular convictions of each author or the particular situations in which the churches found themselves in that period of the oral tradition, critical scholars agree that the gospels contain phrases, stories, and pithy sayings which manifestly come from a creative personality; and this personality can be confidently identified with Jesus of Nazareth.

It is abundantly clear that Jesus' principal challenge was precisely to the self-righteous and disapproving, the class of people characterised in the Parable of the Pharisee and the Tax

Collector[11] – cartoon characters, both of them (as has been said), rather as City financiers have been characterised as "Fat Cats". What better picture of the constricting *persona* has ever been drawn than in this brief story? "God, I thank thee that I am not like other men, extortioners, unjust, adulterers, or even like this tax collector. I fast twice a week, I give tithes of all I get." The identifying of this *persona* with one's real Self is an illusion, crippling the whole of a person's life, their attitude to themselves, to other people, and, if religious, to God.

In view of Freud's contention that religion *per se* is an illusion (and undoubtedly much religious practice does appear to have the effect of fostering illusion), it is important to insist that Jesus, like the Buddha, was concerned *to break through illusion* and to awaken people to reality, for each in his own way recognised, as Erich Fromm has written, "that the great enemies of humanity are those who put it to sleep, and it does not matter whether their sleeping potion is the worship of God or that of the Golden Calf."[12] Another parable provides a brilliant picture of the false self whose illusoriness Jesus was so concerned to unmask. In it the righteous elder brother reproaches his father for the welcome he has laid on for his prodigal younger son. "Lo, these many years I have served you, and I never disobeyed your command; yet you never gave me a kid, that I might make merry with my friends. But when this son of yours (note – not "this brother of mine"!) came, who has devoured your living with harlots, you killed for him the fatted calf."[13] 1900 years before Freud, those words – the resentment they convey towards the father, the repressed envy of his brother's sexual exploits – are as devastating a diagnosis of the "religionist" personality as any to be found in the writings of the father of psychoanalysis.

As we shall see, parables are not analogies; rather this parable is told to administer a kind of shock, leaving all of us who are religious, dutiful and conscientious, as the Pharisees were, with a frowning puzzlement: "You mean, it's better to be a lustful spendthrift?" Or, in the case of the parable of The Labourers in the Vineyard [14], "You mean, those who'd been sweating away the whole day had no right to grumble because those who'd only done half an hour's work received exactly the same pay as them?" Anyone would have sympathy with the grumblers. That is the shock; something equivalent to a Buddhist koan or the thwack on the shoulders of one of his students administered by a Zen master. "Who, or what, is God for you?" Jesus seems to be saying; "one who or which is like a slave owner whose favour must be earned by constant effort, or one whose character is more like that of a loving father, whose love is steady and constant, and whose children have no need to earn his favour because it is there all the time?" – the God, in fact, whose realisation had come to Jesus that day by the river Jordan. We are back to Fromm's distinction between authoritarian and humanistic religion, one which paralyses a person's development or one which furthers it.

The stand taken by Jesus against the "religionists" was obviously of supreme importance to him. One way he expressed the issue was by saying that "No man can serve two masters;"[15] there can be no compromise between the false self and the true Self. And if the purpose of religious revelation is to break through illusion ("reconnection with reality," in E.F. Schumacher's phrase), the hijacking of religion to reinforce illusion ("God, I thank thee that I am not as other men") has to be resisted to the utmost. Perhaps this helps to explain the passion with which Jesus speaks to, and about, the Pharisees. The "Q" source, which as has been seen represents an early collection of traditions, has Jesus saying repeatedly, "Woe to you, scribes and Pharisees." Matthew adds "hypocrites" (the word literally and appropriately means "actors") and generally expands this theme, for reasons which were discussed earlier; all the same, it seems certain that Jesus did use some such words as are found in both Luke and Matthew: "Woe to you Pharisees! for you love the best seat in the synagogues and salutations in the market place." [16] This saying, one of the very few known as "doublets," is found not only in the "Q" source but also in Mark. Then there are those sayings collected by Matthew in what has become known as the "Sermon on the Mount," many of them found also, separately, in Luke. These too are concerned to confront head on the self-righteous *persona* that stifles the true Self and makes individuation, the true development of a human being, impossible. "When you give alms, sound no trumpet before you, as the hypocrites do in the synagogues and in the streets, that they may be praised by men... And when you pray, you must not be like the hypocrites; for they love to pray in the synagogues and at street corners, that they may be seen by men... And when you fast, do not look dismal, like the hypocrites, for they disfigure their faces that their fasting may be seen by men."[17] There could hardly be more devastating warnings to those whose "goal takes the form of God."

Anyone who sets out towards this goal has to be aware that the path they have taken may lead in precisely the opposite direction; it may lead to the boosting of the ego, the false self, rather than to the diminishment of the ego and the fostering of the true Self. And it is true, as Jesus said, that the religious who have been beguiled to take this path "have their reward" in terms of the admiration of others, or a sense of being better than others. The trouble is that the reinforcing of an idealised self-image is no solution to the anxiety and insecurity against which it is a defence. As Erich Fromm observes in his excellent study *To Have or to Be?*, "Because I *can* lose what I have, I am necessarily constantly worried that I *shall* lose what I have." On the other hand, "the anxiety and insecurity engendered by the danger of losing what one has are absent in the being mode. If I am who I am and not what I have, nobody can deprive me of or threaten my security and my sense of identity."[18]

It is in this context that the words with which Jesus concludes these sayings can be understood. "Do not lay up for yourselves treasures on earth, where moth and rust consume and where thieves break in and steal, but lay up for yourselves treasures in heaven, where neither moth nor rust consumes and where thieves do not break through and steal. For where your treasure is, there will your heart be also."[19] Treasures in heaven are the treasures of genuine identity and genuine relatedness, the treasures of the true Self which are the birthright of every person, beside which the treasures of possession and the treasures of the false, idealised self are worthless. So it is no surprise to see linked with this saying those memorable words about the birds of the air and the lilies of the field, followed by the admonition, "Do not be anxious about your life, what you shall eat or what you shall drink, nor about your body, what you shall put on. Is not the life more than food, and the body more than clothing?"[20] Instead, the disciples are urged to "seek first (God's) kingdom, and all those things shall be yours as well." The claims of the true Self are paramount.

The process of switching from illusion – living out an idealised life – to reality is a mystery. For some people a sudden shock seems to bring it about, for others an experience of love or beauty. For most people the initial impetus has to be followed by a long period of assimilation in which the implications of the change are worked out. The word used for this switching process in the teaching of Jesus is repentance. "It implies much more than a change of mind," writes Alan Richardson in *A Theological Word Book of the Bible*; "it involves a whole reorientation of the person-ality."[21] As we have seen, the false self has to be continually reinforced by comparison with others – "God, I thank thee that I am not like other men;" by ticking off a list of moral or religious achievements – "I fast twice a week, I give tithes of all that I get;" or by attracting the admiration or respect of others. Access to the true Self, on the other hand, demands an end to this comparison and this self-righteousness: "Judge not, that you be not judged... First take the log out of your own eye, and then you will see clearly to take the speck out of your brother's eye."[22] Living a truly human life is a natural, unforced expression of this change: "A sound tree cannot bear evil fruit, nor can a bad tree bear good fruit;"[23] to which Luke appends a saying found in a different context in Matthew: "The good man out of the good treasure of his heart produces good, and the evil man out of his evil treasure produces evil; for out of the abundance of the heart the mouth speaks."[24]

Two more characteristics of the teaching of Jesus stand out. First, his teaching is permeated with confidence that the lively life which he lived was, as has been said, a universal birthright. It is the pearl of great price, beside which everything else – money, prestige, a saintly reputation – is as dust. It is treasure, up until now lying hidden but, once found, worth selling everything to obtain.[25] Moreover Jesus appears to have been convinced that to obtain this "real" life was the secret desire of every human being ("The light that lightens every man,"[26] according to the beginning of John's gospel), and that it was his mission to awaken this desire, to affirm and encourage it. "Seek first the kingdom of God;" "Ask, and it will be given you; seek, and you will find; knock, and it will be opened to you."[27] Dig beneath your own hearth and you will find the treasure.

The second characteristic of Jesus' teaching is his repeated warning that this real life cannot be won without cost. Its classic expression is the saying addressed (according to Mark) to "the multitude with his disciples" at Caesarea Philippi: "If any man would come after me, let him deny himself and take up his cross and follow me. For whoever would save his life will lose it; and whoever loses his life for my sake and the gospel's will save it. For what does it profit a man, to gain the whole world and forfeit his life?"[28] This is another example of a "doublet" saying, found in both the Marcan and the "Q" traditions as well as in similar words in John's gospel[29], which shows how central its importance must have been in the teaching of Jesus.

Life lived out of the true Self (characterised by Jesus as "eternal" or "true" life), while it is every person's birthright and secret longing, demands effort and sacrifice; not in the sense of that repression that leads to the diminishment of the personality, but rather as the accomplishment of any art requires commitment, discipline, and painful practice. The motivation is the pearl, the treasure, as the mountaineer's is the summit, the attainment of which is worth every gasping breath and the ever-present fear of falling. As Matthew (following Mark) puts it hyperbolically, "Everyone who has left houses or brothers or sisters or father or mother or children or lands, for my name's sake, will receive a hundredfold, and inherit eternal life;"[30] by which is meant, of course, real (as opposed to illusory) life in this world, not "life after death."

The following pages discuss the parables and miracles of Jesus. The reader may feel, particularly following the detailed attention given to the gospels in the preceding chapter, that it is time to move on to the end of the gospel story, namely the death and resurrection of Jesus. If this is the case, the following two sections, on the parables and miracles of Jesus, can be returned to later, and the reader can go straight to the section "Arrest and Crucifixion".

The Parables

There is, it seems, within everyone a mysterious faculty within the brain hungering to be engaged by story. It appears in the very early years of childhood, and responds eagerly to fairy tales and legends. The Old Testament is full of memorable stories which grip the imagination – the story of Noah and his ark, Joseph and his brothers, David and Goliath, Elijah and the ravens. Within the classical tradition there are the great Homeric sagas of the Iliad and the Odyssey. Within the European tradition there are Grimm's fairytales, the saga of Beowulf, and many more.

The parabolic method appears to be deeply rooted in human

consciousness as a means of implanting the kind of knowledge that is necessary for any growth towards maturity. Writing of the *nkumbi*, the boys' initiation school among a remote people in the Central African jungle, the anthropologist Colin Turnbull describes how "boys are taught in riddles, in songs and dances, where the inner meaning is carefully hidden so that each boy has to discover it for himself, and so discover truth *within* himself."[31]

It may not be altogether fanciful to compare parables to dreams. "Both dreams and stories," writes Anthony Stevens in *Private Myths: Dreams and Dreaming*, "are special in that they act as bridges between two realms of being – inner and outer, Self and environment – integrating them into more up-to-the-minute and better adapted patterns of responsiveness."[32] Having their origin in imagination, dreams and parables need the engagement of imagination to enable them to contribute creatively to the recipient's life. Rollo May compares dreams (and the same could be said of parables) to the utterances of the Delphic oracle in ancient Greece, which "were not to be received passively; *the recipients had to 'live' themselves into the message.*" Their purpose is to "open up new areas of psychic reality, shake us out of our customary ruts, and throw light on a new segment of our lives."[33] This is almost identical to the comment of the influential Dutch Roman Catholic scholar Edward Schillebeckx on the parables of Jesus. "Parables open up new and different potentialities for living, often in contrast with our conventional ways of behaving... (They) point not to another, supranatural world but to a new potentiality within this world of ours: to a real possibility of coming to see life and the world, and to experience them, in a way quite different from the one we are accustomed to."[34] They are a call, in fact, to repentance, to "a whole reorientation of the personality." And Schillebeeckx goes on to make the extremely important point that "originally, drawing a conclusion is left to the listener."[35]

Judaism, it seems, has had a particular bent for using stories as a means for conveying religious truth. The tale to which reference is made from time to time in this book is one of a collection of tales, parables, handed down from Hasidic teachers in Eastern Europe in the eighteenth century. But religious truth is not an end in itself, as Martin Buber insists in his *Hasidism and Modern Man*: "Man cannot approach the divine by reaching beyond the human; he can approach him through becoming human. To become human is what he, this individual man, has been created for. This, so it seems to me, is the core of Hasidic life and of Hasidic teaching."[36] It is the core, too, of the life and teaching of Jesus.

An example from the Hebrew Bible, the Old Testament, illustrates this same rich seam of Jewish parabolic teaching. Its context is the confrontation between the prophet Nathan and King David after the latter's scandalous adultery with Bathsheba and the even more scandalously contrived killing of her husband. The scene is one of the most dramatic in the Bible. David's ruse to get rid of Uriah has been successful, the mourning rituals have been observed, Bathsheba has become his wife and mother of his son. But just when all appears to have gone according to plan the awkward prophet arrives, is admitted, and tells his story: a poor man's one little ewe lamb, which "used to eat of his morsel, and drink from his cup, and lie in his bosom, and it was like a daughter to him," is seized and killed by a wealthy landowner who "had very many flocks and herds," to provide dinner for his guest. As the story unfolds David's sympathy is engaged: "As the Lord lives, the man who has done this deserves to die." But then, looking up, he becomes aware of the prophet's eyes boring into his soul: "Thou art the man."[37]

The purpose of parables, then, is to act as bridges between outer and inner; to enable the listeners, like the boys at the *nkumbi*, to discover truth within themselves. So we have to get rid of the idea that Jesus was using parables to make people more religious – out goes the old idea that they are "earthly stories with a heavenly meaning." "Jesus spoke to men of flesh and blood," wrote the great German New Testament scholar Joachim Jeremias; "he addressed himself to the situation of the moment. Each of the parables has a definite historical setting."[38] It was this definite historical setting that Jeremias set out to discover in his book *The Parables of Jesus*. Of the gospel parables, probably the best known is the parable of the Good Samaritan[39], one of the fourteen found only in Luke. As with Nathan's parable, it appears in Luke as a response to a particular person in a particular situation: a lawyer (here again we have a cartoon character), asking about the characteristics of the life of "the age to come." On being assured that he already knows the answer in the command to love God and his neighbour, the lawyer asks further, "Who is my neighbour?" This is the question to which the parable is a response, one in which the lawyer cannot help becoming imaginatively – one could say emotionally – involved; he cannot help giving his approval to the action of the Samaritan, even though his head tells him (as John's gospel says) that "Jews have no dealings with Samaritans."[40] It is this imaginative engagement that will stay with him long after the encounter is over, prodding him into questioning his presuppositions, and inviting him to look at life from a different angle – to see, in fact, new potentialities for living.

Second only in familiarity to the parable of the Good Samaritan – and again found only in Luke – is the parable of the Prodigal Son[41], to which we now return. The context given to the parable by Luke – the murmuring of Pharisees and scribes at Jesus' association with "sinners" – exactly fits the situation of Jesus' ministry. As with Nathan's parable, the skill of its telling lies in the way it engages the hearers' sympathy, almost against their will. Who could fail to be moved by the picture of the compassionate father running to embrace his errant son, calling for robe and ring and fatted calf? But then comes the sting in the tail, the elder son standing on his morality and refusing to join in his brother's welcome home. Truly, as Buber observed, "if there is nothing that can so hide the face of our fellow-man as morality can, religion can hide from us as nothing else the face of God."[42] Religion, indeed, can be an extremely effective way of entrenching self-centredness – all the more effective for the way it can mask its true purpose. A symptom of this can be seen in the title that the Church came to give to the parable, "The Prodigal Son," turning its message into a call for sinners to repent, rather than focusing on the religious themselves and the warning of Jesus: "Why do you see the speck that is in your brother's eye, but do not notice the log that is in your own eye?"[43] It would have been truer to the original intention of the parable if it had been given the title "The Elder Son".

A striking feature of several of the parables found in Luke, including the two already discussed, is their use of a pair of contrasting characters; they can be found also in the parables of The Rich Man and Lazarus and The Pharisee and the Tax Collector.[44] In all four parables an upright, religious character is set alongside an outsider. Were these parables preserved *because* they favoured the outsider – a figure to the early Christians representing the Gentiles? This may well be so; but they also illustrate Jesus' acute awareness of the truth of Buber's remark about morality and religion quoted above. Certainly the high profile the gospels give to Jesus' controversies with the religious establishment reflects the Jewish authorities' opposition to the Christian movement of a later time; nonetheless, as we saw in the last chapter, his vehement denunciations can be discerned in the earliest strands of the tradition. In this respect, incidentally, Jesus did not stand alone. Setting Jesus within the context of first-century charismatic Judaism, Vermes writes: "The charismatics' informal familiarity with God and confidence in the efficacity of their words was… deeply disliked by those whose authority derived from established channels."[45] On both sides friction was likely to have been felt and it is not surprising that Jesus' harshest words should have been directed at those whose religion denied rather than liberated their humanity and sought to impose that denial on others. "You shut the kingdom of heaven against men; for you neither enter yourselves, nor allow those who would enter to go in."[46] William Blake's poem *The Garden of Love*, with its "chapel ...where I used to play on the green," makes exactly the same charge against the established religion of eighteenth-century England.

And the gates of this chapel were shut,
And 'Thou shalt not' writ over the door;
So I turned to the garden of Love
That so many sweet flowers bore;

And I saw it was filled with graves
And Tomb stones where flowers should be;
And priests in black gowns were walking their rounds,
And binding with briars my joys and desires.[47]

Other parables address the question (touched on in the last section), Where does true wealth lie? Mark's account of the rich man running up to Jesus to ask him, "What must I do to inherit eternal life?";[48] Luke's account of the complainant who said to Jesus, "Teacher, bid my brother divide the inheritance with me,"[49] and Jesus' insistence that "a man's life does not consist in the abundance of possessions,"[50] show that this was as pressing a concern in first-century Palestine where relative poverty was the norm as in twenty-first-century Europe and America where relative wealth is (or is perceived to be) the norm. The two Lucan parables of The Rich Fool and The Rich Man and Lazarus[51] specifically address this issue.

Before leaving the subject of parables, it is worth remembering that it is now universally agreed that the stories and sayings found in the gospels which were selected by the authors

– perhaps from a collection – came to them separated from their original context. We have seen how Matthew and Luke differ in the context and meaning they give to the parable of The Lost Sheep. Since the authors of the gospels were themselves writing for particular people in particular situations, it is not surprising to find that they took the words of Jesus and applied them to those people in those situations, and it is only comparatively recently that scholars have been able to distinguish between the use made of these parables by the gospel writers, and the use made of them by Jesus. The parable of The Sower[52] – the first to be found in Mark's gospel – provides an excellent example. It is followed by an "explanation" which turns the parable into an allegory in which the "meaning" of the seed hovers uncertainly between being the word of God and being the person responding to it. This simply does not fit in with the clarity and directness which appear to be the mark of Jesus' authentic teaching. But there is another clue which makes the interpretation suspect. The reference to tribulation and persecution arising on account of the word[53] does not fit the context of Jesus' ministry; but it *does* fit the context of the early Christian community. It is not hard to imagine a little group of Christians who have seen their numbers dwindle as the original enthusiasm of some wears off, and fear of their orthodox Jewish neighbours persuades others to stay at home, asking themselves: "What is the point of going on?" And how natural for their pastor, using words handed down from the Master himself, to assure them that those who hear the word of God, accept it, and let it transform their lives, are indeed the seed bearing much fruit. Within the context of the lifetime of Jesus, however, the questions must have been completely different. In fact we know what they were: "Where did this man get all this?... Is not this the carpenter, the son of Mary and brother of James and Joses and Judas and Simon, and are not his sisters here with us?"[54] Certainly there was something compelling and innately authoritative about the way Jesus spoke – well captured, incidentally, in Pullman's telling of the Jesus story. But how insignificant was this itinerant preacher with his dozen fishermen disciples, compared with the organised, trained, disciplined clergy of the Jewish establishment – priests, Pharisees, rabbis! Some such questioning as this is what Jesus appears to be addressing in this parable. Rooted in the conviction arising out of his baptism, taking his stand in the tradition of David – young, inexperienced, utterly insignificant beside his much more impressive brothers, and yet anointed by Samuel to become the greatest king the Jews ever had[55] – Jesus pursues his calling. He "is full of confidence," writes Jeremias; "he knows that God has made a beginning, bringing with it a harvest of reward beyond all asking or conceiving. In spite of every failure the Kingdom of God comes at last."[56] Cast into the ground and buried, how can the pathetically insignificant grains of seed ever lead to a crop large enough to feed a family for a year? Drought, patches of infertile soil, the predations of birds and the ruthless competition of weeds are enough to make it appear that the sower's work is a waste of time. And yet...

The process of trying to extricate the parables from the setting and application given to them by the early Christian community (and, of course, by preachers today) is hardly necessary, curiously enough, in the case of those fourteen parables found only in Luke. No doubt they too were used by the community and applied to the situations in which it found itself, but on the whole there is no attempt here, as there is with the parable of The Sower, at allegorical interpretation; nor are there the kind of discordances seen in Matthew's (as opposed to Luke's) version of the Great Supper[57], in which a guest invited straight from the streets is then thrown out for being improperly dressed!

Modern readers will also, like the early Christian community, want to see how a particular parable may relate to their own situation; but it needs to be borne in mind first that they are illustrations of the way Jesus confronted the people among whom he was moving in his own time and the way he opened up to his listeners with their own particular needs and questions "new and different potentialities for living." This may have some bearing upon the way they can be understood in the particular and very different needs and questions with which the twenty-first-century reader is concerned.

The Miracles

We need to recognise at the outset that the miracles of Jesus, impressive and even convincing to previous generations, are today an embarrassment. Fundamentalists' insistence that Jesus' miracles, culminating in the Resurrection, prove their claims about him is wholly inconsistent with the undogmatic, critical, truth-pursuing spirit of our age. Miracles, in short, belong to a first-century world view, along with spirits evil and benign. They do not belong to a twenty-first-century world view, and if Christianity is to be available to this culture, to serve it and contribute to it, it must "incarnate" itself within it. To insist on the literal actuality of the Virgin Birth and the Bodily Resurrection, the Walking on the Water and the Feeding of the Multitudes, is to preclude any serious possibility of engaging with the search for a contemporary spirituality. As the Cambridge theologian Don Cupitt has observed, "A nostalgic realist theology, whose spiritual life is far too narrow and which has lost the original breadth of the idea of God, is functioning as a theology of decline. Decline created it, and it in turn perpetuates the decline."[58]

What, then, of Jesus' miracles? The account of a "miraculous healing" in modern India, told by the writer Charlie Pye-Smith[59], may help to clarify the issues. When he visited the College of the Sacred Heart at Shillong, Pye-Smith was told that the College felt it had a twofold task: first, to be a centre of learning – it was proud to be officially recognised as part of the University of Rome; and second, to take seriously its mission to the tribal people, the Khasi, in whose midst it had been placed. Among other things this included a "ministry of healing," and each morning one of the priests (Fr. Sngi, himself a Khasi but educated in the West) held a kind of surgery for people from the surrounding area. To it, one morning, came a blind woman led by two others. Pye-Smith describes what happened.

After discussing the case quietly with her two companions the priest took the woman's head in his hands and started to speak to her in a loud voice. "She began to tremble and the other women watched apprehensively. He said a prayer, then he withdrew his hands and slapped her several times across the cheek, quite hard, and spat at her forehead. The action was accompanied by more indignant, insistent speech. He then picked up the plastic jug from his table and hurled handfuls of holy water at the woman's face. She bowed her head, but Father Sngi pulled it up again and splashed more water into her eyes. By the time the woman left five minutes' later her eyes were beginning to focus. She was able to make out the shape of the water jug, held up for her to identify, and to count Fr. Sngi's raised fingers."[60] After receiving a further blessing, the woman left with her two escorts and the priest explained to the author what he had done. "This woman – she's a very good woman – her husband has committed adultery and the shock has blinded her. You see, the Khasis believe that adultery will bring sickness and sometimes blindness. It's all psychological. But now she's beginning to see again. Soon she will be fine... I sent the guilt out of her, and I've told it to go to her husband."[61]

Was this "healing," and the others that followed, Khasi or Christian in origin, Pye-Smith asked the priest. "'It's both,' he replied. 'First I talk in a language they understand. By that I don't just mean Khasi, but in terms they understand. But Christ is there, of course. It is Christ who drives out their fears, their ailments.'"[62]

The similarity of this scene to those described in the gospels, the healing of the blind man at Bethsaida in Mark 8: 22-26 for example, is obvious, for the culture in which Jesus performed his healings in first-century Palestine was almost identical to that of the Khasis today – and both utterly remote from our own. Insofar, then, as Christianity has a part to play in the soul-healing of people in contemporary secular Western culture, it has no choice but to talk in a language belonging to that culture; and to recognise that its language (not just words, but terms and ideas behind words) is completely different from that of twenty-first-century Khasis or first-century Galileans. Coming to terms with Jesus as "primarily a miracle-worker" involves facing up to three things. First, the healing miracles of Jesus were not unique, but belonged to a definite strand within first-century Judaism; second, Jesus did not perform miracles, according to the gospels, to create belief in himself; and third, there is a general consensus among biblical scholars that some miracles – the Walking on the Water for example, or the Feeding of the Five Thousand – have been "written up" by the early Christian communities in the light of their reflections on the impact made by Jesus upon them, explained in terms of his "Resurrection". In other words they were cast in such a way as to express certain beliefs about Jesus in terms of the ideas of the culture of that time and place.

First, then, miracles have to be seen in their historical context, that is to say first-century Judaism and in particular (as has already been noted) to that strand within first-century Judaism described by Vermes as "charismatic,"[63] in contrast to the formal, priestly, rabbinic Judaism of the "establishment." The two were not *necessarily* opposed; indeed, says Vermes, "contemporary Jewish thought reserved a place in the fight against evil for the spontaneous and unscripted activity of the holy man."[64] But there was always the potential for this spontaneous and unscripted activity to cause embarrassment. The archetype of this kind of holy man was Elijah, as we saw in the last chapter, and there are several hints in the gospels, apart from Luke's story of the raising of the widow's son, which suggest that an association was made not only between John the Baptist and Elijah, but between Jesus and Elijah.[65] Such an association between Jesus and Elijah would have been completely natural in the northern part of Judea, or Galilee, from which both came. Another such "holy man" contemporary with Jesus was Hanina ben Dosa, whose life (according to Vermes) shows remarkable similarities to that of Jesus, including long periods of prayer to his Father in heaven, a life of poverty, and healings. There is no justification, then, for pointing to the miracles as evidence of Jesus' uniqueness.

Second, there is strong evidence within the tradition, both in Mark and in "Q", that Jesus himself refused to "give a sign," i.e. perform a miracle, when challenged to prove his credentials.[66] Although he certainly seems to have been convinced that his healing work was one of the signs that God's kingdom was being ushered in, "Jesus did not wish to rest his case on his miracles…, since miracles in and of themselves prove nothing."[67]

Now for the third consideration, the likelihood that some of the miracles have been "told up" in the course of the transmission of the tradition (almost certainly before it was written down), to express certain beliefs about Jesus in terms of the culture of the time. The Feeding of the Multitudes, for example, must have had a particular hold on the imaginations of the early Christians, for it is the only miracle recorded in all four gospels – and twice over, with different numbers, in two of them. Barnabas Lindars speaks for most scholars in his comment on John's version of the miraculous feeding: "Whether there was a miraculous element about it or not, the story has been *remembered* for its symbolical importance."[68] Like Fr. Sngi entering imaginatively and sympathetically into the symbolical world of the Khasis, we have to do our best to enter the symbolical world of the early Christians to appreciate why this story gripped their imaginations.

It has to be repeated that the "mindset" of those earliest members of the Jesus movement was formed within the mould of the Jewish Bible. And once again it is almost certain that those two, by now familiar, figures, Elijah and Moses, help to explain something of the symbolical importance of the miracle. In fact, the first story concerns Elijah's successor, the similarly named Elisha.

II Kings 4: 42-44
A man came from Baal-shalishah, bringing the man of God bread of the first fruits, twenty loaves of barley, and fresh ears of grain in his sack. And Elisha said, "Give to the men, that they may eat." But his servant said, "How am I to set this before a hundred men?" So he repeated, "Give then to the men, that they may eat, for thus says the LORD, 'They shall eat and have some left.'" So he set it before them. And they ate, and had some left, according to the word of the LORD.

Exodus 16: 1-3, 11-12
All the congregation of the people of Israel came to the wilderness of Sin, which is between Elim and Sinai... (and they) murmured against Moses and Aaron in the wilderness, and said to them, "Would that we had died by the hand of the LORD in the land of Egypt, when we sat by the fleshpots and ate bread to the full; for you have brought us out into this wilderness to kill the whole assembly with hunger."

And the LORD said to Moses, "I have heard the murmurings of the people of Israel; say to them, 'At twilight you shall eat flesh, and in the morning you shall be filled with bread; then you shall know that I am the LORD your God.'"

This story of God's miraculous feeding of his people in the wilderness forms part of the epic of the Exodus, that great "foundation myth" rehearsed every year by the Jewish people at

Passover. Such is the primal necessity of food that it is not surprising that it should find a place here; nor that, when they came to picture the kingdom God would one day establish on earth, they should imagine a "messianic banquet," a glorious feast for the people of God over which the Messiah would preside after their centuries of want and tribulation. These are the stories and ideas that help to explain the significance, within an early Jewish Christian milieu, of the Feeding of the Multitudes. We cannot recover "what really happened," the original event. What we can recover from this story is a picture of the appeal of Jesus to the imagination of his early followers. Almost certainly the significance of the actual feeding event (whatever it was that took place) did not dawn on them until after the much greater experience which they described as the Resurrection, to be discussed in the next section. By this time the story carried the further resonance of its association with the words of Jesus at the Last Supper, and their familiar rehearsal in "the breaking of bread," the earliest name for the Eucharist (or Mass or Holy Communion, as it was later to become). Only then, as they looked back on those events of which they had been eyewitnesses in their three-year companionship with Jesus, did they begin to see them in a new light; and in this new light Jesus came to be seen as the new Moses, the new Elijah (or Elisha). The healings, the exorcisms, the feedings, were told not just as those of Hanina ben Dosa might have been told, but in the light of the disciples' later conviction: "He has been raised."

Some awareness of this process is essential if we are to be true both to our own twenty-first-century mindset and to that of the gospel writers. The conclusion which modern, critical scholarship has reached is that Jesus did certainly perform the kind of exorcisms and cures familiar to the culture to which he belonged; and secondly that many of the miracle stories have been affected by what can be called the "post-Easter" experiences of the early groups of Christians who passed the stories on. Perhaps no more than this can be said about miracles. And yet it is in the miracle stories that some of the "myth-motifs" of the gospels are to be found, and if one accepts with Jung the role that myth – the language of the imagination – still plays in the lives of contemporary human beings, it may be that the miracle stories, like the parables, can still exercise an appeal complementary to that of the more direct teaching. Hunger and thirst, sickness and health, birth and death, these are all archetypal images; as such they stand for those sets of forces within us to which Abraham Maslow has drawn our attention. On this reading, the entombed Lazarus, "his hands and feet bound with bandages, and his face wrapped with a cloth," is Everyman; and it is to each one of us, called "towards wholeness of self…, toward full functioning of all (our) capacities," that Christ cries with a loud voice, "Come out!"[69] With this in mind we may now turn to the story of the death and resurrection of Jesus.

Arrest and Crucifixion

The "stereoscopic" kind of approach to the miracle stories that was suggested in the last section, that is to say the harnessing of both reason and imagination, is equally necessary in reading the gospel accounts of the passion, death, and resurrection of Jesus. It is no longer possible to say that every detail of the arrest, trial, and crucifixion of Jesus as recorded in the gospels is factually, historically true. We have seen how the scriptures of the Jewish bible themselves became a source for part of the passion story. Fact and interpretation became welded together at a very early stage of the Jesus movement. This was inevitable, for those first Christians were convinced of two things: first, that even though Jesus had been put to death with at least the acquiescence of their own religious authorities, he had in fact been innocent; and second, that in their actual experience of him "risen from the dead" their scriptures seemed to make sense as they had never done before. His death and resurrection (for so they talked about it), far from contradicting or jarring with the scriptures, seemed now to fulfil them. Some years before the earliest gospel was written, Paul wrote to the Christians of Corinth to remind them that he had "delivered to you as of first importance what I also received, that Christ died for our sins in accordance with the scriptures, that he was buried, that he was raised on the third day in accordance with the scriptures."[70] So this conviction about the fulfilment of the scriptures was there, right from the beginning, and it inevitably surfaces from time to time in the gospels themselves, as we have already seen – most clearly in Luke, where the author paints a picture of the risen Jesus speaking to his disciples: "'These are my words which I spoke to you, while I was still with you, that everything written about me in the law of Moses and the prophets and the psalms must be fulfilled.' Then he opened their minds to understand the scriptures."[71] This was the conviction they felt impelled to announce to their fellow Jews, most of whom could not get beyond the fact that Jesus had been condemned to death by their own leaders, even if they had left it to the occupying power to carry out the sentence.

As for the actual events that led up to the crucifixion, we have already seen that there was, built into the relationship between religious establishment and charismatic prophet a mutual suspicion; the growing hostility to which that led in the case of Jesus, as it is portrayed in the gospels, has a ring of truth. What seems to have finally lit the fuse was almost certainly the action of Jesus overthrowing the tables of the moneychangers in the temple, coupled with some such words as are reported in Mark's gospel, addressed to the disciples: "Do you see these great buildings? There will not be left here one stone upon another, that will not be thrown down."[72] As Sanders comments: "The action and the saying, in the view of the authorities, constituted a prophetic threat;"[73] and this seems to have been the immediate cause of Jesus' arrest.

The earliest sources of the tradition (Mark and "Q") agree that an essential ingredient of Jesus' preaching was that with him God's kingdom – that to which the Jewish people had come to look forward with ever greater urgency – was being ushered in, and that its complete realisation lay in the near future. Something has been said about this already, and we shall return to the subject when we come to consider the petition for the coming of the kingdom in the Lord's Prayer. It will be remembered that the Qumran community by the Dead Sea regarded its mission precisely in terms of preparing for the coming of the kingdom, and Jesus' insistence that it was about to arrive, coupled with his provocative words and dramatic actions in the temple, would have been dynamite in a city already bursting at the seams with excitable crowds of pilgrims.

The high priest, Caiaphas, had the responsibility for preserving order in the Jewish homeland, and in particular in the holy city. A major disorder would have certainly provoked an immediate and bloody response by the Roman army, and at all costs Caiaphas had to prevent this. "To keep his job," writes Sanders, "he had to keep control."[74] Furthermore, to prevent not only present but also future trouble, Jesus had to be permanently eliminated. The remark John puts into the mouth of the high priest expresses the point exactly: "It is expedient that one man should die for the people, and that the whole nation should not perish."[75] There appears to have been some debate within the High Priest's Council how this should be carried out. In the case of blasphemy, Jewish Law made provision for death by stoning, and Luke's second volume, Acts, asserts that this was the punishment meted out to Stephen. The fact that Jesus was not put to death by this means suggests that although this was the ostensible charge against him, for some reason the Council (perhaps they could not agree) handed him over to the Roman occupying power – on a political charge (according to the Council claiming to be "King of the Jews", without question a treasonable claim in the eyes of Rome). In any event Jesus was handed over to the Roman governor, Pilate, with sufficient evidence to make sure that he did what had to be done.

Once again it has to be repeated that the gospels – and their sources – are products of the period in which they were written, and that in them is reflected the bitterness, on both sides, of the separation of the Christian movement from orthodox Judaism. Scholars suggest that they also show signs of exonerating the Romans from blame for the death of Jesus. Against the evidence of Philo and Josephus, two contemporary Jewish sources, that Pilate was a cruel, sadistic governor, the gospels portray him as an unwilling victim of Jewish pressure, inwardly convinced of Jesus' innocence. It is far more likely that he had Jesus executed immediately the case was brought before him, showing as little hesitation in the case of Jesus as he had done in the cases of his other victims. The reason for this curious "adjustment" of the truth may well be not only the desire to put all the blame on the Jewish authorities whose successors had recently excommunicated the Christian movement, but also to persuade the Roman authorities that it had never been seen as a threat by those authorities, that they had been unwilling to crucify its founder, and that it should be granted the same legal exemptions (be declared a *religio licita*) as Judaism.

Resurrection

So much for the death of Jesus: what of its sequel? The most obvious sequel is that the Jesus story did not come to an end with his death. At some point the disciples were shaken out of despair and disillusion, and began to form a movement whose marks were, apparently, energy and joy. "That Jesus' followers (and later Paul) had resurrection experiences is, in my judgement, a fact. What the reality was that gave rise to the experiences I do not know,"[76] declares Sanders. What then to make of the resurrection stories?

The earliest written reference to the resurrection occurs in Paul's letter to the Corinthians quoted above. This merely records that Jesus "was raised", and that he appeared to Peter, "then to the twelve. Then he appeared to more than five hundred brethren at one time, most of whom are still alive, though some have fallen asleep. Then he appeared to James, then to all the apostles. Last of all, as to one untimely born, he appeared also to me."[77] (It is worth noting, incidentally, that just as Paul makes no reference to the birth, virgin or otherwise, of Jesus, so he makes no mention of the disciples coming to the tomb and finding it empty – an indication, probably, that that part of the story had not yet been incorporated into the tradition.) No information is given about how he "appeared", and Paul makes no distinction between Jesus' appearance to the first disciples (according to the gospels within days of the crucifixion) and to himself, some three years' later. The "Q" tradition appears to have no resurrection story at all. When the tradition surfaces next in the gospel of Mark we have an account that tells of the women going to the tomb, finding it empty, and being addressed by "a young man, sitting on the right side, dressed in a white robe." This young man (who by the time Luke's gospel came to be written had become "two men in dazzling apparel", upgraded to "an angel" in Matthew, and "two angels" in John) then addressed them: "You seek Jesus of Nazareth, who was crucified. He has risen, he is not here."[78] So a comparison of Mark's account with those of Matthew, Luke, and John, shows how the tradition had become further developed, the different versions, according to Professor C.F. Evans, serving "as different interpretations of the resurrection."[79] And lest this judgement be seen as the conclusion of a maverick scholar, out of step with "orthodox" Christian scholarship, none other than the world-renowned (but officially denounced) Roman Catholic theologian, Hans Küng, maintains that "it is hardly possible... to refute the assumption that the stories of the tomb are *legendary elaborations of the message of the resurrection.*"[80]

We have seen how the gospel writers incorporated into their works material from the traditions available to them – some obviously very early. It is therefore just possible that there are traces in Luke and John of an early tradition maintaining that the earthly body of Jesus, now lying in the grave, was of no significance. "Why do you seek the living among the dead?"[81] the women in Luke are asked, while in John the risen Christ, appearing in bodily form to Mary Magdalene, says (in the New English Bible translation), "Do not cling to me."[82] Far from trying to reconcile the accounts, we need to recognise that here, as with the birth stories, we are being addressed in the language of myth; and the purpose of the myth is to move those who read or listen to the gospel away from concentration on the physical presence of Jesus to his spiritual presence within them. This seems to have been the purpose of Paul's assertion to the Christians at Corinth, that "even though we once regarded Christ from a human point of view, we regard him thus no longer."[83] Are these sayings, perhaps, evidence of a tendency among some of the earliest believers to look towards (perhaps also to revere and even make pilgrimage to) the tomb of Jesus, and of the insistence of the disciples or other leaders of the earliest Christian community that the presence of Jesus was not in the tomb, but within themselves? This at any rate is the conclusion of Geza Vermes. "The conviction of the spiritual presence of the living Jesus accounts for the resurgence of the Jesus movement after the crucifixion."[84] With this verdict Edward Schillebeeckx agrees. "The experience of having their cowardice and want of faith forgiven them, an experience further illuminated by what they were able to remember of the general tenor of Jesus' life on earth, thus became the matrix in which faith in Jesus as the risen One was brought to birth. They all of a sudden 'saw' it."[85]

"He is not here;" "Do not cling to me;" and St. Paul's comment, which I remembered in the old Authorized Bible translation, "though we have known Christ after the flesh, yet now henceforth know we him no more;" these three sayings kept coming back to me between the time of my beloved wife's death, and her funeral. An hour earlier "she had been here", but not now. "In the flesh" I would know her no more, but of course my whole being clung to her, and it took a long time for that clinging to subside, and to live in the present without her physical presence; and it took a longer time still to know with utter conviction that who and what I was now had been transformed by our life together, and did not depend upon that physical presence. In that sense, though I continue to carry her photograph around with me, her Real Presence is within me, and for me this experience helped to illuminate the gospel narrative.

There remain two further stories to consider that belong to the resurrection traditions. At the beginning of his second volume, Acts, Luke tells of the risen Jesus staying with his disciples for a period of forty days, "speaking of the kingdom of God," and telling them that they would shortly be "baptized with the Holy Spirit."[86] At the end of this period, "as they were looking on, he was lifted up, and a cloud took him out of their sight."[87] None of the gospels mentions such a definite end to the resurrection appearances (that to Paul, as we have seen, occurring some three years' later). Does this story belong with others to an "Elijah tradition," echoing the Elijah epic's account of the end of the great prophet's life, when, as he was taken up to heaven by a whirlwind, he bequeathed his spirit to his disciple Elisha?[88] The Acts story certainly appears to symbolise the transition between the time when the disciples were learners dependent on the physical presence of Jesus, and the time when they went out on their own, convinced that the spirit which they had seen at work in Jesus was now at work in them. The second story (celebrated by the Church as Whitsun or Pentecost) draws out the theme of the passing of Jesus' spirit to the disciples. Luke represents it as an event taking place fifty days after Easter, in which "suddenly a sound came from heaven like the rush of a mighty wind, and it filled all the house where they were sitting. And there appeared to them tongues as of fire, distributed and resting on each of them. And they were all filled with the Holy Spirit."[89] Here the mythical element is plain, and comes from a very different tradition from that drawn on by the author of John's gospel, in which Jesus appears to his disciples on the day of his resurrection, breathes on them, and says "Peace be with you. As the Father has sent me, even so I send you… Receive the Holy Spirit."[90]

"Whenever the poetry of myth is interpreted as biography, history, or science, it is killed. The living images become only remote facts of a distant time… Furthermore, it is never difficult to demonstrate that as science and history mythology is absurd."[91] Passionate defence of the bodily resurrection of Jesus is utterly misguided, when what is needed, and needed urgently, is the recovery of respect for myth – in this case the age-old, world-wide myth of death and rebirth, of death as the condition of rebirth. This is the myth of which Christ, in Western traditional culture, is the supreme archetype. From the very earliest days, it seems, this myth was given expression in that "rite of passage" which John the Baptist had performed for his fellow Jews and for Jesus himself, for whom, as we have seen, it became a turning point. It expressed, physically and brilliantly, as the person was plunged under the water and then "raised up" again, the death and rebirth that life continually demands if it is to be life in all its fullness. As Paul wrote to the Christians in Rome: "Do you not know that all of us who have been baptized into Christ Jesus were baptized into his death? We were buried therefore with him by baptism into death, so that as Christ was raised from the dead by the glory of the Father, we too might walk in newness of life."[92]

The American philosopher Jacob Needleman, reflecting on the way that the previously living images of Christianity have become little more than "remote facts" in modern Western culture, concludes that there is only one way to recover those lost images, namely "to bring back Christianity as a guide to the search for ourselves."[93] We are back, it seems, to the story of the rabbi standing at the bridge in Prague. And it may be that it is just here that the great death and rebirth archetype, symbolised so powerfully in the crucifixion and resurrection of Christ, can begin, in Campbell's words, to "bring into play the vital energies of the whole human psyche." What is it, after all, that is impeding humankind in its slow growth towards *monanthropism* but its seeming inability to die to past certainties? Better to hold on to the clear delineations of *apartheid*, the rigidities of the Reformation, the infallibilities of Pope or Bible, and all those identities which offered security in the past than to risk losing all for an impossible hope. And what we see, so intractable, in the world outside ourselves, is no less true within our own inside world, for as Robin Skynner has observed, "the more fundamental the impending change, the more it must feel to us like a threatened dissolution and loss of everything that really matters to us, everything we most essentially feel we are."[94]

"There is no question," Joseph Campbell reminds us: "the psychological dangers through which earlier generations were guided by the symbols and spiritual exercises of their mythological and religious inheritance, we today (in so far as we are unbelievers, or, if believers, in so far as our inherited beliefs fail to represent the real problems of contemporary life) must face alone, or at best, with only tentative, impromptu, and not very effective guidance."[95] In the final chapter of this book an attempt will be made to sketch out a very brief (and certainly tentative) outline of the kind of way in which the resources contained within Christianity might be made available to twenty-first-century human beings in their search for wholeness and for the realisation of the unity of the human race. It is only if the myth can be appropriated that we shall discover whether there might be something more than dead ashes beneath the hearth of our own home.

Chapter 4

Appropriating the Myth

Right Effort, Right Contemplation

"A passionate longing to grow, to be, is what we need,"[1] wrote Teilhard de Chardin in 1941. Myth affirms this longing, as we have seen Joseph Campbell insist, by supplying "the symbols that carry the human spirit forward, in counteraction to those other constant human fantasies that tend to tie it back." This is why myth is important, neither "fairy stories for children", nor untruth. Returning to Britain from years spent in Africa, the distinguished Roman Catholic priest and theologian Father Adrian Hastings was immediately conscious of the "myth-starved" culture of Europe and America, compared with the "myth-rich" culture of Africa. "What we need is not de-mythologising," he wrote, "but re-mythologising, a rebirth of images rather than their consistent elimination."[2]

From the very earliest times, some 300 years before they began celebrating Christmas, Christians gathered to celebrate the death and resurrection of Christ. It was an affirmation of the central Jewish rite of Passover, with its own powerful resonances – the departure from Egypt, the crossing of the Red Sea, the 40 years in the desert, and the arrival in the Promised Land. This was the myth to which the death and resurrection of Christ had given new impetus: "Unless a grain of wheat falls into the earth and dies, it remains alone; but if it dies, it bears much fruit."[3] In so celebrating it, they displayed a profound awareness of the fundamental human dilemma: to cling to safety and defensiveness out of fear, or to go forward into the abyss which turns out to be the path to wholeness. "He who loves his life loses it." The early Christians seem to have been so convinced that these words contained the kernel of Christ's teaching, and expressed the significance of his death, that (as was pointed out in chapter three) it is the only saying of Jesus recorded in all of the three separate traditions represented in the gospels, Mark, "Q" and John.[4]

The Christian myth cannot be separated from the Jewish myth of which (in its own eyes) it was an expression, and out of which it had grown. The Jesus portrayed in the gospels is one whose whole formation was moulded by the mythology of his people. Luke's picture of him in the Temple at the age of twelve, "sitting among the teachers, listening to them and asking them questions,"[5] represents Jesus not just passively accepting that mythology but actively engaging with it and later illuminating it for those who had chosen to follow him: "then he opened their minds to understand the scriptures."[6] It was instrumental in carrying his spirit forward to a new realisation of being human, in which the divisive classifications of saint and sinner, Jew and Gentile, male and female, dropped away; a realisation, in fact, of *monanthropism*. Paul, for all Philip Pullman's distaste, grasped this fundamental point. "There is neither Jew nor Greek, there is neither slave nor free, there is neither male nor female; for you are all one in Christ Jesus."[7] More than any other gospel, Luke emphasises the contrast between the vibrant, "realised" humanity of Jesus and the tense, defensive, judgemental timidity of his opponents. Thus he became, in Luke's words, "a light for revelation to the Gentiles, and for glory to thy people Israel."[8]

Like any member of his people, Jesus must have absorbed its mythology by attendance at the synagogue and by exposure to its great legends: of Abraham, "who went out, not knowing where he was to go;"[9] of Jacob, the younger son renamed Israel, "for you have striven with God, and with men, and have prevailed;"[10] of Joseph, left for dead by his brothers, yet becoming their saviour; of Moses, who "endured as seeing him who is invisible,"[11] and of all those other heroes catalogued by the Epistle to the Hebrews who "won strength out of weakness."[12] Year by year Jesus must have re-lived with his people the drama of Passover night; week by week, as dusk began to fall on Friday evenings, participated in the lighting of the Sabbath candles and the blessings over wine and bread. In Matthew's gospel is to be found the great parable of The Sheep and the Goats, with its invitation, "Come, O blessed of my Father, inherit the kingdom prepared for you from the foundation of the world; for I was hungry and you gave me food, I was thirsty and you gave me drink, I was a stranger and you welcomed me, I was naked and you clothed me, I was sick and you visited me, I was in prison and you came to me."[13] Here we see the fruit of profound reflection on those solemn words at the end of the book of Isaiah: "Is not this the fast I choose: …to let the oppressed go free, and to break every yoke? Is it not to share your bread with the hungry, and to bring the homeless poor into your house; when you see the naked, to cover him, and not to hide yourself from your own flesh?"[14] It would hardly be overstating the case to say that without what Roszak called "the master ideas, the moral and metaphysical paradigms"[15] contained in the scriptures and liturgies of his people it would not have been possible for a Jesus to emerge. They provided the essential food of his imagination.

Never to have been exposed to such experience is undoubtedly an impoverishment, and perhaps contributes to our clinging with greater fervour to decaying myths and degraded images. It deprives us of noble "images to think with," and of a noble standard by which we might be able to take charge of our lives. Yet simply "going to church" no longer provides an adequate answer for most people in our "post-Christian" world, for it does not seem to connect with their – with our – own experience. The late Dom Bede Griffiths, a Benedictine monk who spent the latter part of his life in India, seeking to open himself to all that he felt Hindu spirituality had to offer to the West and to a Christianity that had become so enmeshed in past Western culture as to become blind to its original thrust, recognised this. "The structure of doctrine and ritual and organisation which (the Church) has inherited are no longer adequate to express the Divine Mystery, like those of Israel at the time of Christ."[16] What new and more adequate structures will emerge in which the great Christian myth might be communally celebrated we do not yet know, but the community at Taizé provides an inspiring example. If this myth is to enter into the bloodstream of modern culture, there have to be those who are prepared to engage with it, "to become ritually and ethically involved with it, and allow it to effect a profound change"[17] in their lives. Not many people will see the point of this kind of engagement, or feel the need for it, but it is without doubt a task to be undertaken by "the religious whose goal takes the form of God". They will need to heed the wise advice of the great German theologian Rudolf Otto, coming from nearly a hundred years ago, commenting on the "proposed recastings" of the Lutheran liturgy that were then being considered. "In these," cautions Otto, "we find... nothing unaccountable, and for that reason suggestive; nothing accidental, and for that reason pregnant in meaning; nothing that rises from the deeps below consciousness to break the rounded unity of the wonted disposition, and thereby point to a unity of a higher order – in a word, little that is really spiritual."[18]

The huge decline in church attendance that has taken place over the last half century is partly a sign of the inadequacy to which Dom Bede pointed – an inadequacy which is not removed by translating from Latin to English, or "*thees* and *thous*" into "*yous*". It is also a response to our prevailing secular culture. Yet those of us who have settled comfortably into this culture might perhaps consider some questions which on the whole go unasked. Does the closure of pubs and cinemas that has also gathered pace in this period symbolise a retreat from the social, from community, to individualism? We can drink at home, watch DVDs at home. But is something lost? Perhaps the crowds who attend football matches have something to say about the human need for community, the experience of togetherness, the sharing of a common focus and the ecstatic expression of emotion? This kind of communal activity undoubtedly reaches parts of human experience that watching the game in front of a television (or drinking alone at home) does not. Is not religious experience attenuated if it does not include some such communal celebration? Is it not in the community of any religion that the myth is preserved, celebrated, and handed on? Reflecting on this I find myself led back to communal worship, in spite of its inadequacies. The churches need to reclaim something of the ecstasy of the football stadiums, a need which Pentecostal churches seem to meet. "*Ambuye, alengele lisungu! Kriste, alengele lisungu!*" – the wholehearted singing of a congregation of Malawian migrant mineworkers for whom I celebrated the Eucharist at a copper mine on the banks of the Limpopo 50 years ago lives with me still. Their singing of the *Kyrie*, like their singing of the hymns, with no organ and no hymn books, was uplifting, and it is hardly surprising that African and Caribbean people often turn to Pentecostal forms of worship rather than what must seem to them the insipid worship of the "white" churches.

But how *can* we still engage in Christian worship when Jesus has been shown to be a "mere" man, who did not walk on water and did not physically rise from the dead? Certainly we cannot if myth is equated with untruth. Our argument has been, however, that myth is a way of expressing truth; it is the language of imagination rather than intellect. As we saw Karen Armstrong insist earlier, it is about "enabling us to live more intensely in the world." In seeing Jesus wholly – and uniquely – living out what it meant to be a son of God, the earliest Christians referred to him as *the* Son of God. In the course of time, as Geza Vermes has shown in his book *Christian Beginnings*,[19] this ascription became a title and a dogma. But we can now understand this ascription as an archetype: Jesus as the archetypal son/daughter of God; directing our attention to him, as Buddhists do to Gautama, can affect us in our struggle to become human. "To all who received him, who believed in his name, he gave power to become children of God."[20] "All who are led by the Spirit of God are sons of God... When we cry, 'Abba! Father!' it is the Spirit himself bearing witness with our spirit that we are children of God, and if children, then heirs, heirs of God and fellow heirs with Christ," Christ who is later described as being "the first-born among many brethren."[21] This is the myth to set beside, and to question, the seductive and enervating myth of capitalist consumerism, for it is a mistake to imagine that because we have abandoned religion we do not live by myth, something of which the makers of advertisements are well aware.

A further point needs to be made. Those who deny that the Virgin Birth, the Resurrection, the Walking on the Water, the Raising of Lazarus and other miracles are literal, historical, physical facts are described by "traditionalists" as "reductive", traitors undermining Christianity from within. So it was in 1860 with the publication by seven Anglican scholars of *Essays and Reviews*, expressing their belief in the necessity of free inquiry in religious matters, and in particular accepting the findings of the new critical approach to the first five books of the Old Testament. Two of the authors were deprived of their livings and 11,000 clergy issued a declaration affirming their belief in the inerrancy of Scripture and in eternal punishment. So it was again in 1889 when another group of Anglican scholars published *Lux Mundi*, whose purpose, in their words, was "to put the Catholic faith into its right relation to modern intellectual and moral problems". Today the conclusions of both books are almost universally accepted, except by Creationists who share the "either/or" approach of atheists and continue to see Adam and Eve as historical figures. If the presence, and the value, of myth in the Old Testament is accepted, why not also in the New Testament? What is needed is not denial of myth, but glad acceptance, the "re-mythologising" and "rebirth of images" for which Adrian

Hastings has pleaded. This is not easy when for so long myth – "mere myth" – has come to be seen as *un*truth, rather than, as we saw Nicolas Berdyaev putting it earlier, a medium which "expresses life better than abstract thought can do," bringing together "two worlds symbolically."

As well as some kind of participation in the on-going communal worship of the Church, however, there are two other ways of appropriating the Christian myth which are immediately realisable: study of the gospels and private prayer.

The purpose of studying the gospels is to educate us out of inadequate images of Jesus – either as believers or as non-believers – which we may never have questioned; to gain an understanding of his teaching; and to apprehend how he expressed that teaching in his own life. If it is to be undertaken, it must be undertaken with some awareness of the methods used and the conclusions reached by modern biblical scholarship. It is simply not good enough to exclude spirituality from the scientific outlook we assume in every other department of our lives. Commentaries on all four gospels are readily available, but as a general introduction to the gospels E.P. Sanders' *The Historical Figure of Jesus* cannot be bettered. Mark, as we have seen, was the earliest to achieve written form (it is also the shortest), so his gospel would be a good place to begin, with some awareness by now of its make-up, and of its mixture of "myth" and "fact". This might be followed by a study of Luke, which as well as containing a large part of Mark and the traditions associated with the "Q" source contains a unique collection of parables, and beautiful versions of the Birth and Resurrection stories. Next, both as a contrast and as an introduction to a very different kind of gospel, might come the deeply reflective passages to be found in chapters 13 to 17 of the Gospel of John.

The gospels do not provide instructions for living but rather food for the imagination and a kind of reference point outside ourselves, our time, and our culture. Marion Milner, to whom reference has been made earlier in this book, found herself gradually becoming aware that "the gospel story is concerned, not with morals at all, not with what one OUGHT to do, because someone (God, father) expects it of you, but with practical rules for creative thinking, a handbook for the process of perceiving the facts of one's own experience."[22] Milner goes on to liken the gospel story to a Chinese puzzle-box; you have to learn the trick of getting inside it to come upon its treasures, and the key lies in an understanding of the importance of myth and symbol – of inner meaning. The fundamentalist, taking the gospel literally, values the outside of the puzzle-box and presents that as the treasure. The cheerful atheist also sees only the outside of the puzzle-box and sends it spinning into the waste paper basket. Those who sit uncomfortably between these two positions see the gospels as a resource which gives our minds something to engage with, assumptions and aspirations to which otherwise we might be blind. In this way they can become part of that "dialogue with the past" whose purpose, as Karen Armstrong has put it (see the introduction), is to enable us "to find a perspective from which to view the present." It is because they come from a culture remote from our own that the perplexities with which they confront the modern reader make an up-to-date commentary essential. Even so, parts (like the "Little Apocalypse" in Mark 13) will remain obscure and of little or no value, and it cannot be pretended otherwise. Nevertheless, as it is hoped the previous chapters will have shown, enough remains to make the gospels a resource of timeless importance. Some may want to go further and turn to the sagas which moulded the imagination of Jesus, and the prophets and psalms which inspired him. These also can provide for the contemporary reader a rich resource for the imagination (though much here will also be ungraspable), as well as leading to a deeper understanding and appreciation of the gospels.

We turn now to the second way of appropriating the Christian myth. 80 years or so ago the Russian philosopher Nicolas

Berdyaev remarked that "the sort of Christianity which is purely outward in character and never rises above the level of mediocrity is today on the decline; while that which possesses eternal significance and an inner mystical quality is growing more intense and stronger."[23] The present widespread interest in "spirituality" which finds expression in attendance at meditation classes, retreats, or in courses to learn about Buddhism or Sufism, confirms Berdyaev's view. It is as though after years of turning our attention to activity, to the outer, there were now a hunger for the inner and a recognition that here there is work to be done which can no longer be evaded. It is a work to which the mystics of every religion have been alive, but which now, it seems, many more are called to share. It is what is represented in the last injunction of the Buddhists' Eightfold Path as "Right Contemplation." In the Christian tradition (according to Evelyn Underhill's great study of mysticism) this work involves "the stripping off of the I, the Me, the Mine... (and) self-abandonment to the direction of a larger Will."[24] In the words of her fellow-Anglican John Taylor, deeply influenced like Adrian Hastings by time spent in Africa (including a night in a canoe on Lake Victoria, working with a team of roving fishermen), prayer is resistance "against the tyranny of false values, a resistance against the pressures of quick decisions, superficial opinions, unexamined fears, a resistance against the complex web of influences that tightens around us... It is a fight for freedom, our own and that of others, an antidote against illusion and escapism and alienation, a struggle for human space and human ways of living."[25] It is an instrument, above all, in the long, painful struggle out of self-centredness, which is the first essential step on the road towards *monanthropism*.

The gospel traditions leave no room for doubt that for Jesus this inward activity was of the highest importance, was indeed the very condition of his outward effectiveness. "He withdrew to the wilderness and prayed."[26] "He went out into the hills to pray;

and all night he continued in prayer to God."[27] Nor can there be any doubt both that his disciples understood this ("Lord, teach us to pray"[28]), and that Jesus was as adamant in stressing for his disciples as for himself the need to pray: "When you pray, go into your room and shut the door and pray to your father who is in secret."[29] Prayer, so far from being a retreat into illusion, is the means of breaking out of illusion, including the illusion of the Santa Claus God, and reconnecting with reality. Each person who arrives at the conclusion that this is in fact a worthwhile activity has to work out the practical details, what to do when you "go into your room and shut the door." Some find sitting in the lotus position helpful; some like to kneel; others (I am one) find sitting in an upright chair, spine straight – perhaps with a pad in the small of the back – the position most conducive to the activity of prayer.

Acting on a hunch that this inward activity might be accessible to anyone, I decided to put it to the test with a class of fifteen-year-olds. They were, in the euphemistic jargon, a "challenging" group, and to be allotted them for the last two lessons on a Friday afternoon was a daunting prospect. The previous term, when every classroom was being decorated for Christmas, they had offered to decorate mine. When I came in to inspect the result, it was immediately apparent that the balloons either side of the blackboard came from Boots the Chemist rather than from the usual supplier of balloons, and with grins all round I asked them to remove them. On this particular Friday afternoon Buddhism was the subject, and Right Contemplation the particular topic. I told the students to push the desks to the side of the room, and then either to lie on the floor, or sit on a chair. I told them that the purpose of the exercise was to "centre down", to be completely still and to become aware of a level within themselves to which the noise and bustle of school (and home) normally denied them access. I challenged them to see if they could do it, without talking or fidgeting, for a few minutes.

Quietly I guided them from the tips of their toes to the tops of their heads, concentrating on their breathing, helping them to "centre down". To my amazement, there was utter silence in that room for a full ten minutes, finally broken by a giggler who found himself rounded on by the rest of the class. Now this was hardly Buddhist contemplation, or Christian meditation; but it was perhaps an introduction to an area within themselves of which they had been unaware, a hint that prayer, in one form or another, was not an activity to be confined to monks and nuns.

The disciples' question, "Lord, teach us to pray," must of course have been a question asked from the very beginning by those caught up in the Jesus movement; and it is clear that the answer given by Jesus, what came to be known as "The Lord's Prayer," was soon regarded as definitive. It belongs, like so much of the teaching of Jesus, to the "Q" tradition, and the shorter version of it which appears in Luke's gospel is believed by many scholars to be the more primitive. While the prayer could well have been the prayer of any first-century – indeed of any modern – Jew, it obviously achieved its special status by reason of its association with him whose self-understanding was expressed specifically in terms of Son in relation to Father. It represents the response of Jesus to the primal experience of his baptism: "Thou art my beloved Son; with thee I am well pleased." Surely it was with this in mind that Paul wrote to the Christians in Rome, "When we cry 'Abba! Father!' it is the Spirit himself bearing witness that we (too) are the children of God."[30]

The Lord's Prayer: I

Prayer (to return to Karen Armstrong's phrase) is a means of reaching down to "the deeper regions of the psyche." It belongs to the realm of imagination and, as has been suggested, is a means of relating the truths of myth to one's own life. But this does not mean that intellect and rational thinking can be discarded. Because the Lord's Prayer is part of the teaching of

Jesus it has to be understood in the context both of that teaching and of his life and death. Nevertheless the distinction made in the Noble Eightfold Path of Buddhist tradition between "Right Mindfulness" and "Right Contemplation" is a valid one. Prayer demands the stilling of discursive thinking and openness to the "Transcendent Self," which in terms of the Christian mythology is expressed as the call of the Father within.

The term "Father" raises the question whether it can be an appropriate one for people to use in the twenty-first century. Freud's explanation of the tyrannical superego (Erich Fromm's "authoritarian conscience") as an internalising of the punishing father rings true enough to experience for it to be taken with the utmost seriousness by anyone reflecting on religious practice. But the question has also to be asked whether it is possible, particularly for women, to continue to use the term "Father" in an age which has come to appreciate the necessity for both sexes of using language which is inclusive. It is obviously possible, for example, to add to Paul's words to Christians in Rome, "You have received the spirit of sonship,"[31] the words "and daughtership." Would it be appropriate to pray "Our Mother" as a symbol of the Transcendent Self? If this better expresses a sense of loved-ness, and therefore "sister-ness" to every other human being, then to my mind it is just as valid as "Our Father". In any case, no one reading the gospels could possibly conclude that the Father who appears to have been the focus of Jesus' imagination has any connection with the forbidding, all-powerful figure of Freudian analysis. Unfortunately such a figure is frequently the burden of the religious today as it was for those cartoon Pharisees featured in the gospels; it can be detected in the respectable dullness and censoriousness, often accompanied by a kind of saccharine sweetness, of those within its grip. This kind of Father, and the infantile dependence which it fosters, has to be let go of if any real growth is to take place. "It seems to me," wrote Jung to the Protestant pastor who was later to officiate at his funeral, "that only the man who seeks to realise his own humanity does God's will, but not those who take to flight before the bad fact 'man', and precipitately turn back to the Father, or have never left the Father's house. To become man is evidently God's desire in us.... God has quite obviously not chosen for sons those who hang on to him as the Father, but those who have found the courage to stand on their own feet."[32] The God who demands abasement or dependence is utterly at odds with the spontaneity and joie-de-vivre which shines out of the character of Jesus in all the gospel traditions, and it is impossible to imagine how his supremely unauthoritarian style of teaching could have issued out of communion with such an internalised figure. On the other hand, it matches exactly the image of the father so beautifully portrayed in the parable of the Prodigal Son.

The reflections that follow may be regarded as, at best, extremely tentative illustrations rather than instructions or models of how using the Lord's Prayer as the basis of contemplation may be as valid and meaningful an activity today as in any age in the past.

Our Father, who art in heaven, hallowed be thy name
To the question "Who am I?" a whole range of answers is possible: the child of my parents, inheritor of their physical and psychological strengths and frailties; the product of my culture, my class, my environment, my education; a consumer, the target of all those siren voices urging me to find more life by acquiring more things or more experiences. Each of these answers can form a possible basis on which to build my life, something lodging in the imagination as a reference point which will inform my attitudes and relationships. The opening words of the prayer – Our Father/Mother – present a different possibility, the basis on which at least from the age of 30 Jesus of Nazareth lived his life. The record of the gospels, scant though it is, gives some idea of how this particular reference point shaped his relationship to

religion, to himself, and to other people. Every encounter – with the fishermen who became disciples, with tax collectors, with street women, with the religiously orthodox, with the sick and the crazed – was a putting to the test of his baptismal conviction, a hallowing of his own name as son, and therefore brother.

In terms of the Christian mythology, the alternative to hallowing the Father's name is hallowing the ego or the false self. As we have seen, the false self encourages illusion, and the purpose of prayer is to break out of illusion and wake up to reality. "The truth will make you free,"[33] says Jesus to his disciples in John's gospel. Here the Buddhist and Christian diagnoses of the human condition coincide. "Individuals are in bondage to their desires which control them and keep them in a state of illusion. Until this can be accepted and until there is a wish to overcome this state of affairs, bondage will continue. The Buddha emphasised that the path to the wisdom that can begin this journey is a long and hard one that few will wish to undertake... Through meditation the individual frees him or herself from distractions and from the limitations imposed by the ego."[34] Jesus' words preserved in a "Q" saying make exactly the same point: "The gate is narrow and the way is hard, that leads to life, and those who find it are few."[35]

Dwelling on this opening aspiration of the Lord's Prayer – "Father, hallowed be thy name," as it is in Luke's more compressed, and for us perhaps more accessible, version[36] – is the first step on the path to wisdom and to freedom. In the space or spaces set aside each day for prayer, whoever commits her or himself to the long, hard journey cultivates the stillness that is the essential condition for becoming aware of that other voice so insistently drowned out by the "white noise" of the clamouring ego. If our life's task is to loosen the hold of those forces within us which cling to safety and to open ourselves to wholeness of self, then the "Our Father" supplies a personal metaphor for that which is calling us toward the growth of our own true personhood; and personhood appears to be the goal towards which the whole thrust of evolution has been working as if in a long process of yearning. Jesus, from his baptism onwards, took on himself the experiment of living out his sonship/brothership; that is the same experiment that we take on in this prayer, with all the implications it may have for the way we see ourselves and those whom we come across. In these first two words of the Lord's Prayer monotheism and *monanthropism* meet.

Thy kingdom come
If the prayer's first petition reflects on the true status and goal of the person praying, the second petition looks forward to its fullest expression and fulfilment. The individual is inseparable from the species; the task of realising one's own individuality is inseparable from that of transcending it and arriving at the experience of universality. If the kingdom of God in Jesus' teaching had an individual dimension, it had also, as for every Jew, a social dimension: community under the rule of God. His view of this aspect of the kingdom differed from that of the Zealots because it included Gentiles, even Romans and the Jewish tax collectors who worked for them; differed too from that of the Pharisees (or at least of the unfair caricatures of the Pharisees we find in the gospels) because it included "sinners". His relations with other human beings, as recorded in the gospels, demonstrate his conception of this aspect of God's kingdom. Without doubt, as we have seen in the parable of the Sheep and the Goats, it came to him from his reflection on the great Jewish prophets. Another example from an earlier chapter in Isaiah will serve to illustrate his ecstatic image of the kingdom of God.

Isaiah 11: 6-9
The wolf shall dwell with the lamb, and the leopard shall lie down with the kid, and the calf and lion and the fatling

together, and a little child shall lead them. The cow and the bear shall feed; their young shall lie down together; and the lion shall eat straw like the ox. The sucking child shall play over the hole of the asp, and the weaned child shall put his hand on the adder's den. They shall not hurt or destroy in all my holy mountain.

It was with this passage in mind that Alan Paton, author of *Cry the Beloved Country* and noble leader of the non-racial Liberal Party of South Africa in the *apartheid* years, entitled the first volume of his autobiography *Towards the Mountain.* In it he describes a moment when he himself caught the vision of the "holy mountain," the vision which his Christian faith taught him to see as the vision of Jesus. It was at the funeral of Edith Jones, wife of one of the founders of the South African Institute of Race Relations. "I was overwhelmed. I was seeing a vision, which was never to leave me… In that church one was able to see, beyond any possibility of doubt, that what this woman had striven for was the highest and best kind of thing that anyone could strive for in a country like South Africa. I knew then that I would never again be able to think primarily in terms of race and nationality. *I was no longer a white person, but a member of the human race."*[37]

Becoming aware of oneself as "a member of the human race," getting some kind of glimpse of the kingdom, cannot help bringing into view all the inequalities and injustices that are contrary to the kingdom. Only a very few will feel called to respond to that glimpse by entering politics (though it is important that some should), but each person has to decide which of the many other paths, however small, she or he will have to take towards the realisation of the kingdom in the course of their own pilgrimage towards the holy mountain, towards *monanthropism.* The petition is also an act of affirmation that in a world riven by wars and communal strife, the kingdom is there, a buried seed, making its appearance every so often as slavery is abolished, women achieve the vote, weapons are decommissioned. It might have been the text for President Obama's unscripted talk to Democrats in the House of Representatives the day before the American healthcare vote: "Every once in a while a moment comes where you have a chance to vindicate all those best hopes that you had about yourself, about this country, where you had a chance to make good on those promises you made… We are not bound to win, but we are bound to be true. We are not bound to succeed, but we are bound to let whatever light we have shine."[38]

Thy will be done, on earth as it is in heaven
This phrase is not in Luke's version of the prayer, so may well have been inserted by Matthew. Nevertheless it is entirely appropriate to the spirit of the prayer, reflecting as it does the words of Jesus in the Garden of Gethsemane the night before his death: "Abba, Father, all things are possible for thee; remove this cup from me; yet not what I will, but what thou wilt."[39] Resting in the affirmation of who we truly are, reaching out both to our own completion and to the completion of that kingdom of which we are part, the third petition might be seen as opening up to us the implications of the first two; one of which is certainly that life cannot be won without cost.

In the first three gospels the paradigm for this process is presented in the story of the "Temptations". Following immediately the ecstatic experience of Jesus at his baptism, he is portrayed spending time (the mythological number of forty days, the number of years, in his people's myth, that they had spent in the desert between leaving Egypt and entering the Promised Land) working out what he is to do about it. The mythical "wild beasts" in Mark's account are replaced by the three proposals put to Jesus by the devil in the more elaborate mythological account preserved in the "Q" tradition.[40] Similar accounts of agonising wrestling are told in connection with the decisive "calls" both of the Buddha and Muhammad – the Buddha assailed by the hosts of Mara, the Evil One, as he sat under the bodhi or pipal tree, Muhammad terrified as he awoke from his great vision in the cave. In every case the struggle is between the claims of the two sets of forces, the ego and the true Self. Each person has to discover what, for them, is the will of the Father, and then *to take appropriate action*. Failure to do so, following instead the will of the ego, the false self, will result in the deadening of the personality and other symptoms.

The same principle applies in the social sphere. It is easy enough to assume that "they" who run things are acting for the best, and to surrender to inertia. Organisations like the World Development Movement in Britain perform a great service in exposing the ways in which particular businesses, or national or international policies, may in fact serve to perpetuate injustice. Other organisations campaign against the arms trade and its disastrous role in fuelling conflict in the developing world; or against the blight of homelessness and poor housing; or against the use of torture and the abuse of human rights. All these, and many more, are reminders of the infinite dimensions of praying "OUR Father." "Thy will be done" must involve some kind of commitment, in whatever sphere one may choose, to align oneself with those who are striving for the kingdom, wrestling with poverty and injustice, rather than with those whose interest lies in their perpetuation; in fact with those who want to further, rather than to resist, the realisation of the unity of the human race of which the kingdom of God is the symbol.

The first three petitions of the Lord's Prayer – "Thy name be hallowed, thy kingdom come, thy will be done" – involve a stilling of the mind and a reaching out to the true Self symbolised by the Father. Only then does the prayer, in its remaining four petitions, turn to "us".

The Lord's Prayer: II

If prayer involves "the stripping off of the I and self-abandonment to the direction of a larger Will," it is hardly surprising that the first three petitions of the Lord's Prayer are focused on that larger Will of which "Our Father" is a metaphor. Only then will the concerns of the ego be able to be seen in their proper perspective.

Give us this day our daily bread

Hearing this phrase, Jesus' disciples, all Jews, would have instantly recalled an episode in their own great Deliverance myth, the Exodus. During their people's forty years' wandering in the wilderness they had been mysteriously provided with bread daily, and on the day before Sabbath with enough for the morrow as well.[41] The story contrasts the anxious murmuring of the Israelites, longing to go back to "the fleshpots of Egypt," with the faithfulness of God in providing for their needs. And so the disciples might also have associated with these words the admonition of Jesus about anxiety: "Do not be anxious about your life, what you shall eat, nor about your body, what you shall put on. For life is more than food, and the body more than clothing. Consider the ravens: they neither sow nor reap, they have neither storehouse nor barn, and yet God feeds them."[42]

A treasured memory recorded by Viktor Frankl from his time in Auschwitz suggests that "bread" symbolises more than itself. "I remember how one day a foreman secretly gave me a piece of bread which I knew he must have saved from his breakfast ration. It was far more than the small piece of bread which moved me to tears at that time. It was the human "something" which this man also gave to me – the word and the look which accompanied the gift."[43] So one praying this prayer at the beginning of the day might look forward with hope to all that the day may bring, and at the end of the day might look back in gratitude to all that it has given. There is no better cure for resentment, and perhaps no greater contribution to our sense of well-being, than gratitude, and this petition in the Lord's Prayer provides a good space to reflect on all the ways in which delight has come to us. Those whose temperament leads them naturally to dwell on the negative cannot escape their temperament; but gradually, through practice, they may become more alive to the possibility of finding manna in their wilderness, even if through nothing more than a meeting of eyes with a stranger in the street. Nor is it only from other people that unexpected delight may come: in his wonderfully evocative book *The Wild Places* Robert Macfarlane gives other examples: "a sparrowhawk sculling low over a garden or street, or the fall of evening light on a stone, or a pigeon feather caught on a strand of spider's silk, and twirling in mid-air like a magic trick. Daily, people were brought to sudden states of awe by encounters such as these: encounters whose power to move us was beyond expression but also beyond denial."[44] Add to these the sudden bursting-in upon the senses of the scent of honeysuckle or coffee, a passage in a book or something on television or radio which has us exploding in laughter; these, too, are daily bread. Towards all of them we can be open and for all of them we can be grateful.

Forgive us our trespasses as we forgive those who trespass against us
As much as (perhaps more than) any other religion, Christianity has been associated with guilt; and yet it is only towards the end of the Lord's Prayer that there is any mention of sin. A narrative contained in the gospel of Luke (already referred to in chapter two) may help to distinguish the meaning of sin as it was understood by Jesus from that notion which has been such a disfigurement of Christianity. Once again it involves a Pharisee, whom we can now recognise as an archetype of the superego, the inner voice of the accuser.

Luke 7: 36-50

One of the Pharisees asked him to eat with him, and he went into the Pharisee's house and sat at table. And behold, a woman of the city, who was a sinner, when she learned that he was sitting at table in the Pharisee's house, brought an alabaster flask of ointment, and standing behind him at his feet, weeping, she began to wet his feet with her tears, and wiped them with the hair of her head, and kissed his feet, and anointed them with the ointment. Now when the Pharisee who had invited him saw it, he said to himself, "If this man were a prophet, he would have known who and what sort of woman she is who is touching him, for she is a sinner." And Jesus answering said to him, "Simon, I have something to say to you." And he answered, "What is it, Teacher?" "A certain creditor had two debtors; one owed five hundred denarii, and the other fifty. When they could not pay, he forgave them both. Now which one will love him more?" Simon answered, "The one, I suppose, to whom he forgave more." And he said to him, "You have judged rightly." Then turning towards the woman he said to Simon, "Do you see this woman? I entered your house, you gave me no water for my feet, but she has wet my feet with her tears and wiped them with her hair. You gave me no kiss, but from the time I came in she has not ceased to kiss my feet. You did not anoint my head with oil, but she has anointed my head with ointment. Therefore I tell you, her sins, which are many, are forgiven, for she loved much; but he who is forgiven little, loves little." Then those who were at table with him began to say among themselves, "Who is this, who even forgives sins?" And he said to the woman, "Your faith has saved you; go in peace."

Here is a direct challenge to the traditional "religious" view of sin, for which Simon the Pharisee speaks. Luke's story suggests that the woman's actions were evidence enough of "a whole reorientation of the personality," brought about, presumably, by her encounter with Jesus. From "missing the mark" (the root meaning of the word used for "trespasses" in Luke's version of the prayer), the woman had found it. She had been recalled to her true Self from the false self by which her previous life had been dictated. So her faith had saved her, while Simon was still in thrall to what the poet W. H. Auden referred to as "the concupiscence of the oppressor."[45] It is here, Jung suggests, that the experience of forgiveness has to begin, in the discovery "that I myself stand in need of the alms of my own kindness – that I myself am the enemy who must be loved."[46]

To pray "forgive us our trespasses," then, is to confront the distinction between the true Self and the false self; at least to aspire to some kind of illumination or awareness of the ways in which we have "missed the mark". It is to recollect, too, all those who by their own self-acceptance have from time to time been the agents by whom we have come to be truly at home with ourselves, recalled to our true Self. According to the gospel traditions it was only when Jesus had arrived at his own Great Awakening that he became the means of awakening others. "Take up your bed and walk;" "Your sins are forgiven;" "Your faith has saved you;" these sayings could only contain healing power because they were spoken by one who had experienced the overwhelming conviction of his baptism: "Thou art my beloved Son; with thee I am well pleased." The petitions in the first half of the Lord's Prayer are all oriented towards affirming that same conviction in the heart of the one using the prayer.

"If you imagine someone who is brave enough to withdraw all (his) projections," wrote Jung, "then you get an individual who is conscious of a considerable shadow... Such a man knows that whatever is wrong with the world is in himself, and if he only learns to deal with his own shadow he has done something for the world."[47] This is the teaching handed down also in the parable of the Moat and the Beam, in the "Q" tradition: "How can you say to your brother, 'Brother, let me take out the speck that is in your eye,' when you yourself do not see the log that is in your own eye?"[48] Simon the Pharisee projected his shadow onto the woman "who was a sinner" (his words); the elder son in the parable projected his onto his younger brother. The authority with which Jesus spoke both to the woman and to Simon is the authority of one who was indeed brave enough to withdraw all his projections. He could be angry without being petulant, gentle without being sentimental. Through much testing he had learned to deal with his own shadow.

A letter of the remarkable American Trappist monk and social critic Thomas Merton to the Muslim scholar Abdul Aziz contains a shrewd analysis of the way in which when others "trespass against us" even our enemies can become, in the Buddhist phrase, "our co-creators". "This attachment to the self is a fertile sowing ground for seeds of blindness, and from this most of our errors proceed... (T)he unjust and unkind actions of others, even though objectionable in themselves, can help us to strip ourselves of interior attachment."[49] As the words and deeds of others, acting out of their false selves, affect us, so do ours affect others. As others "miss the mark", so do we. Only the forgiven can forgive; only the one reunited with her or his true Self can be the means by which others may be reunited to their true Self. It was the gift gratefully accepted by the woman with the alabaster flask, and in the parable of the debtors offered to Simon. It is the greatest gift one human being can offer another – but only, perhaps, if the giver is not conscious of being a giver.

Lead us not into temptation
Jesus' initial time of testing, immediately following his baptism, has already been referred to, a foretaste of that supreme time of testing in the Garden of Gethsemane. This is the kind of testing we pray not to be led into, as a boxer at the start of his career might beg to be excused a bout with a world champion. Yet the crude analogy suggests that it is only by confronting testing now that we shall be able to meet the severer tests that may come

upon us in the future.

It is a strange paradox that although human beings seek comfort, ease and leisure, they also seek challenge, and go out of their way to find some difficulty to pit themselves against. No one *has* to climb Everest, or sail single-handed round the world, abseil down a cliff face, or attempt a difficult crossword. Yet it is as if we knew at an instinctive level that life would be deprived of some essential element if it did not confront us with times of testing. It seems to be an expression of our desire to grow. Perhaps this helps to explain the deep respect we feel for those heroes of the human spirit who have emerged from terrible times of testing with their humanity enlarged rather than diminished: Solzhenitsyn in the gulag; Viktor Frankl and Elie Wiesel in Auschwitz; Brian Keenan in Beirut; Nelson Mandela on Robben Island; and that inspiring and continuing witness to the truth in Burma, Aung San Suu Kyi.

No one, of course, can predict what form their own times of testing will take, only that in one form of another they will certainly come: breakdowns in relationships, the sudden or not so sudden onset of crippling illness or dementia in one's partner or in oneself, the death of dearly loved ones and ultimately one's own death. Before his own ultimate time of testing Jesus prayed, "Father, remove this cup from me," and so will we; but his earlier words to Peter, "Get thee behind me, Satan! For you are not on the side of God, but of men,"[50] show how well aware he was of the fatal cost of evading the testing when to meet it was the only way forward.

A reflection from Nikos Kazantzakis' autobiographical *Report to Greco* may provide a useful illustration of the place of testing in human growth. "Monkeys must have felt the momentum of the universe inside them…, urging them to stand on their hind legs, even though the pain made them howl, and to rub a pair of sticks together to produce a spark, even though the other monkeys derided them. This is how ape man was born, how man was born."[51] It appears to be a principle of life that humanity – our own and that of the species – can only develop by coming through times of testing. The evil from which we pray to be delivered is the siren call to go back, to evade. "The dragon to be slain," writes Joseph Campbell in *The Hero with a Thousand Faces*, "is precisely the monster of the status quo;" therefore "the mythological hero is the champion not of things become but of things becoming."[52] The archetype of that hero is dormant within the imagination of every human being, summoned to fulfil their own personhood, and within the imagination of the human race, summoned towards *monanthropism*. It is the archetype illuminated by Christ's own passage from death to resurrection.

* * *

Writing in 1945 to the Dominican priest Fr. Victor White (whose observations about the relevance of analytical psychology to an understanding of Christian symbols were quoted at the beginning of chapter 3), Jung had this to say: "*It is of the highest importance* that the educated and the 'enlightened' public should know religious truth as a thing living in the human soul and not as an abstruse and unreasonable relic of the past. People must be taught to see where they come in, otherwise you never bridge the gulf between the educated mind and the world of dogmatic ideas... The appalling lack of understanding threatens the Christian religion with complete oblivion. You cannot preach to a man who does not understand the language."[53] For the most part, we are in the same position as that in which the Khasis would have been had Fr. Sngi preached to them in the language of the University of Rome. The reflections on the Lord's Prayer outlined in the last few pages express one person's conviction that its language is indeed translatable into terms of our contemporary experience, and that it can touch our souls in those deeply buried places where mythical archetypes still live. They attempt to show that prayer need not be the meaningless repetition that it has all too frequently become; and that as a means towards contemplation and a "stripping off of the I" it can play a uniquely precious part. It can, as Thomas Merton suggested of the contemplative life, give us a new experience of time: "one's own time, but not dominated by one's own ego and its demands. Hence open to others – *compassionate* time, rooted in the sense of common illusion and in criticism of it."[54]

The chorus of T.S. Eliot's *The Rock* asks three haunting questions:

Where is the Life we have lost in living?
Where is the wisdom we have lost in knowledge?
Where is the knowledge we have lost in information? [55]

"Living and partly living" is a recurring phrase in another of Eliot's choruses,[56] both of which express the sense of what Teilhard referred to as "the *taedium vitae*", the tediousness of life. Prayer provides no simple solution to this tediousness, but perhaps the author of John's gospel, his own life illuminated by long reflection on what Jesus meant by referring to himself as Son in relation to Father, was speaking from experience when he put into the mouth of Jesus these words: "The water that I shall give him shall become in him a spring of water welling up to eternal life."[57]

Not far from St. Paul's Cathedral in London, scene of the long-lasting anti-capitalist protest between 2011 and 2012, there is a street called "Paternoster Row", so called because it was once the street in which craftsmen made rosaries, or "Paternosters". From the beginning, it seems, the Paternoster, the Our Father, has been used by Christians as a means by which they have drawn up living water, a means of contact with the life-giving Self. Fingering the prayer's petitions one by one like the beads of a rosary may be one of the most effective ways of relating the Christian myth to the task of becoming human.

Conclusion

If Robert Byron is right, that human beings' distinction from animals lies in their being endowed with a sense of quest, negligible in some, insistent in others; and if we can identify this sense of quest with Rollo May's "Cry for Myth", then how is it that this sense and this cry seem to go unsatisfied? It is easy enough to blame, as Schumacher does, two centuries of scientific imperialism, but those who have been charged with being the guardians of myth should remember the lesson contained in Jesus' parable of the Mote and the Beam, and look first to their own responsibility for this state of affairs. The clinging to forms which expressed truth in the past but do so no longer and the strident insistence on religious dogmas which take no account of new levels of understanding have done untold damage. The hungry have gone unfed. For many people Christ and Christianity have come to be seen as inextricably tied to a culture which has passed, as irrelevant to our contemporary strivings as the antics of the Greek gods on Mount Olympus.

The vast number of people who have read or seen the films of C.S. Lewis' *Narnia Chronicles*, Tolkien's *Lord of the Rings*, J.K. Rowling's Harry Potter stories, or indeed Philip Pullman's own "Dark Materials" trilogy can be seen as evidence of this hunger seeking satisfaction. The cry for myth is not necessarily the sigh of the oppressed creature in a heartless world. The emergence of myth as humankind emerged from animalkind in the slow, laborious upthrust of evolution, had a purpose, and that was to provide the inner, symbolic language to articulate its yearnings, and a sense of orientation and direction for its upward journey. Myth represented a deposit, a storehouse of wisdom. That storehouse has been there into whatever cultures the human species, as it gradually covered the globe, diverged – a process, incidentally, magnificently illustrated in the BBC/British Museum series of programmes, *A History of the World in a Hundred Objects*. But the triumph of "Logos" (the analytic) over "Mythos" (the imaginative) since the Enlightenment has led to a depreciation of this storehouse of wisdom and a despising of its rich deposit. "The habit of binary thinking," writes John Hick, "has so restricted us to the alternatives of straight fact or straight fiction that we find it difficult to feast on poetry, allowing emotion free rein, rejoicing in the magical powers of the imagination, and glorying in a great mythic story as our human way of relating to that which transcends all human thought."[1] One by one those peoples who continued to live in the light provided by their myths – the Bushmen of Southern Africa, the Aboriginal peoples of Australia, the native Indian peoples of North America – have found themselves overwhelmed by the tidal wave of "Logos" imperialism, with tragic results. A moving picture of this process among the last is supplied by Hugh Brody's fascinating account, *Maps and Dreams*.[2] "The old-timers, the strong dreamers," Brody's informant told him, "knew many things that are not easy to understand. People – white people, young people – yes, they laugh at such skills." And yet the strong dreams of those old-timers provided cohesion to the life of their people and helped them with "that essential knowledge to which ordinary men and women have limited access."[3]

The question has to be squarely faced whether the "essential knowledge" of which the old-timers were the guardians in that North American Indian hunting culture is available to us in our "Logos-dominated" culture. We have seen how the contents of myth, pre-dating modern, scientific culture, were regarded by Sir James Frazer as "mistaken explanations of phenomena," originating in that "instinctive curiosity" which in our time "seeks satisfaction in philosophy and science" (see chapter one). But others since Frazer have come to see that there is more to myth than this. "Every historical man," Mircea Eliade has insisted, "carries on, within himself, a great deal of prehistoric humanity."[4] To be in touch with this neglected aspect of ourselves is "to be able to see the world in its totality."[5] To be out of touch with it – to be ignorant – is falsely to identify "reality with what each one of us *appears to be or to possess.*"[6]

If all this is true, and reality comprises not only what is "out there," to be apprehended by the intellect, but "in here", to be apprehended by the imagination, then it would seem to be important to devote disciplined effort to the cultivation not only of the intellect, but also of the imagination. This involves, first and foremost, the ability to distinguish between the imagination's capacity to be (as Marion Milner put it) "a burrowing mole" from its capacity to be "a hovering kestrel," an instrument either for evading truth or for reaching it. "Truth and delusion, good and evil, are equally possible," wrote Jung not long before he died. "Myth is or can be equivocal, like the oracle of Delphi or like a dream."[7] One of the great contributions Jung has made to modern thought has been his recognition of the vital importance, for the very survival of humankind, of disciplined attention to the unconscious, whose receptor he believed to be imagination and whose language he believed to be myth and symbol.

By giving to Jesus the title "Christ" the first Christians were expressing their own conviction that for them he was of more than historical significance. There was that about Jesus (they seem to have felt) which touched their imagination, and which both appealed to and illuminated the mythology with which it was furnished. For countless millions since then Christianity has continued to provide a structure of meaning. Like all myths, the Christian myth has been pressed into the service of delusion and so contributed to the hideous barbarities of the Crusades, the Inquisition, the persecution of the Jews, the conflicts which continue to disfigure Northern Ireland and other parts of the world. In South Africa it underpinned the whole system of *apartheid*. Then there are "the witch-hunts, the heretic-burnings, the narrow fanatical zeal that comes so swiftly and naturally to some individuals in positions of power when faith gives them an excuse, the sexual perversion of children" to which Philip Pullman points as such utter betrayals of "the good man Jesus"[8]. But it has also served the cause of truth, and found expression (as Pullman acknowledges) in miracles of artistic creation – music, buildings, pictures – as well as in "good works" – schools, hospitals, and the improvement of social conditions.

It has been the contention of this book that if the Christian myth is to serve the cause of truth rather than delusion in contemporary culture and engage critically with it, it has to show itself committed to truth in the way it approaches its own foundation documents, the four gospels. The critical investigation of the Bible was from the beginning part and parcel of that movement which was to lead to such remarkable advances in the understanding of the natural world. Some critical understanding of the nature of the gospels, how they came to be written, their blend of biographical details and myth-motifs, and the picture of Jesus that emerges from them when read in the light of that understanding, would seem to offer the kind of discipline necessary to foster the imagination's quest for truth and to curb its temptation towards evasion.

Yet the subject of Christ's teaching is internal, not external, truth: the "inward possibilities of the species." It is here that the understanding of human nature built up over the past hundred years by the great pioneers – Freud, Adler, Jung – and their successors can provide such help. The Sermon on the Mount, read in the light of their insights, can be seen to be directed not towards making a person religious, but towards making a person human. It was what the Jesus whom they named the Christ represented in his own person, that pellucid life lived in moment-by-moment response to the Father and winning through to resurrection by way of the cross, to which those early believers responded with such conviction; so too with the very core of the Christian myth, the Crucifixion-Resurrection drama, originally celebrated in a single ceremony, not separated, as it later became, into the two separate days of Good Friday and Easter. To this conviction, that here is a new revelation about what it means to be or to become human, the legends they wove about his birth and resurrection bear witness. How, so we may imagine them musing, could we not regard the coming into the world of such an illuminated and illuminating being as a miracle? For similar reasons the Buddhist scriptures recount how the Buddha "did not enter the world in the usual manner, (but) appeared like one descended from the sky;" and again, at his death, how "the heavens were lit up by a preternatural fire."[9] So too, those Christian pioneers may have mused, how could we any longer live in the delusion that life is to be attained by acquisition, when he exemplified in his own person the truth that it is only if a grain of wheat falls into the earth and dies that it can bear much fruit?[10]

This book has argued that Christ is as much (to repeat the awkward but meaningful phrase) the "Paradigm of the Individuating Ego" today as in those early days and in that very different culture in which the gospels were written. But myth has to be apprehended and teaching absorbed. It has to be internalised if it is to do its work in helping us fulfil the potentialities of our species. This is the purpose of the communal worship of the Church, and insofar as it has allowed itself to become insipid it has betrayed that purpose.

It is also the purpose of reading the gospels, and of private prayer. Christ's injunction to "go into your room and shut the door and pray to your Father who is in secret,"[11] and the prayer which the "Q" tradition records as his response to the disciples' request "Lord, teach us to pray," suggest one way by which the internalising process may take place. In prayer the self is reconnected with its source (recalling Schumacher's dictum that "religion is the reconnection of man with reality"). In the face of those beguiling fantasies of which advertising's slogans and pictures are the sacrament, the silent and secret activity behind the shut door puts the imagination in touch with another goal and another path. Prayer offers the possibility of that kind of "lateral thinking" which suddenly apprehends that what the eye at first assumes to be a picture of two white faces looking at each other across a dark space can be seen also as a dark vase standing between two white spaces. To Thomas Merton this was the very raison d'être of the contemplative life. "There is a kind of contagion," he wrote, "that affects the imagination unconsciously much more than we realize. It emanates from things like advertisements and from all the specious fantasies that are thrown at us by commercial society. These fantasies are deliberately intended to exercise a powerful effect on our conscious and subconscious minds. They are directed right at our instincts and appetites, and there is no question but that they exercise a real transforming power on our whole psychic structure. The contemplative life should liberate us from that kind of pressure, which is really a form of tyranny."[12]

So, it was suggested, time spent fingering those six beads of the rosary which is the Paternoster, the Our Father, is time spent on a supremely important activity. Each petition leads the person praying it along a path determined by one who, while deeply immersed in and grateful for the culture of his own people, saw through its temporary illusions to its eternal principles. These are the principles of human living that are as valid in contemporary culture as in that of any previous century in any part of the world. Now as then humankind has before it two possibilities: to cling to safety and defensiveness out of fear, or to venture forward toward wholeness of self; back to the *apartheid* of the cultural and religious forms that separated us, or forward towards *monanthropism*.

Like every other great religion, Christianity has been the repository, and the Church the guardian, of a people's myth. Through its rituals, its fastings and its festivals, that myth has touched the hearts of untold millions, and for many it still does. Today, however, the hearts of many are no longer touched by those rituals. For them – for us – "there is no going back, and one does not know whether going back is always the better way."[13] The only alternative is to go forward, to see (as Richard Holloway has so well put it) "whether we can discover new ways of using the Christian tradition that will deepen our humanity, our care for the earth and for one another."[14] It is a challenge, as another writer has put it, "to develop new forms of faith through which the human spirit can be transformingly related to the Transcendent within the context of our modern knowledge of ourselves and of our environment."[15] Perhaps new groupings and patterns will emerge, as they did within Judaism after the destruction of the Temple and the exile of so many of its people in the sixth century BCE. Perhaps church membership will come to be seen by some as not necessarily lifelong, but as a kind of school for living from which they will move on as they move on from secular schools, once they have incorporated the myth into themselves. This leaves unanswered, of course, the question of how the myth is to be transmitted down the generations, as Judaism did for Jesus and Christianity has done for Christians. This book would not have been written had it not been for that transmission. How this life-enhancing myth might be more vibrantly celebrated is a task with which the Church has constantly to engage, for is not such celebration as vital to the myth's apprehension as silent, personal contemplation?

My hope is that in time answers to these questions will emerge. Meanwhile perhaps, to their mutual surprise and delight, those whose lives are oriented by the Christian tradition might find their hands grasped by others whose lives are oriented by the tradition of Islam, and both will find themselves saying together those inspiring words of the Quran:

God is our Lord and your Lord.

We have our deeds, and you have your deeds;

There is no argument between us and you;

God shall bring us together, and unto Him is the homecoming.[16]

In that pilgrimage into the future they will have to preserve a lightness, and a recognition that those around them who do not share their orientation are nonetheless fellow pilgrims. They will need to remember those wise words of Teilhard de Chardin quoted in chapter two, that "what looks like no more than a hunger for material well-being is in reality a hunger for higher being;" and that for some of those fellow pilgrims who yearn for a spirituality which resonates with their deepest aspirations the treasure might be found much nearer than Varanasi or Bangkok, hidden all the while "beneath the hearth of our own home".

References

Introduction

1. Richard Dawkins: *The God Delusion*. Bantam, 2006.
2. Robert Byron: *The Station*. Century Publishing, 1984. p. 66
3. Karen Armstrong: *A History of God*. Vintage, 1999. p. 351 (italics mine).
4. Laurens van der Post: *The Dark Eye in Africa*. Hogarth Press, 1955.
5. Alfred Adler: *Understanding Human Nature*. Tr. Colin Brett. Oneworld,
   Oxford, 1998. p. 69.

Chapter 1

1. Martin Buber: *Hasidism and Modern Man*. Tr. Maurice Friedman. Harper Torchbooks, 1958. p. 173.
2. Viktor E. Frankl: *Man's Search for Meaning*. Tr. Ilse Lasch. Hodder and Stoughton, 1987. pp. 136-7.
3. Viktor E. Frankl: *Man's Search for Ultimate Meaning*. Insight Books, Plenum Press, New York, 1997. p. 135.
4. Sir James G. Frazer: *Introduction to Apollodorus: The Library*. Heinemann, 1921. p. xxvii.
5. Sigmund Freud: *The Future of an Illusion*. Hogarth Press, 1961. p. 241.
6. N. Berdyaev: *Freedom and Spirit*. Tr. Oliver Fielding Clarke. Geoffrey Bles: Centenary Press, 1935. p. 70.
7. Theodore Roszak: *Where the Wasteland Ends*. Anchor Doubleday, 1973. p. 348.
8. Karen Armstrong: *A Short History of Myth*. Canongate, 2005. pp. 8 and 3.
9. Lewis Mumford: *My Works and Days*. Harcourt Brace Jovanovich, 1080. p. 483.
10. Karl Marx: *Towards a Critique of Hegel's Philosophy of Right*.

Cited in E. Fromm: *Beyond the Chains of Illusion*. Abacus, 1980. p. 105.

11. E. Fromm: *Psychoanalysis and Religion*. Yale University Press, 1950. p. 26.

12. Ib., p. 21.

13. Karen Armstrong: *The Battle for God. Fundamentalism in Judaism, Christianity and Islam*. Harper Collins, 2000.

14. John Hick: *The Fifth Dimension*. Oneworld, Oxford, 1999. p. 238.

15. Ib., p. 100.

16. Richard Dawkins: *Unweaving the Rainbow*. Penguin, 1998.

17. Ib., p. 30.

18. Rhagavan Iyer (ed.): *The Moral and Political Writings of Mahatma Gandhi: Vol. 1*. Oxford University Press, 1986. p.464. See also Stanley Wolpert: *Gandhi's Passion – the Life and Legacy of Mahatma Gandhi* (Oxford University Press, 2001) for an excellent analysis of the difference between the two founding fathers of independent India.

19. Sigmund Freud: *Civilisation and its Discontents*. Hogarth Press, 1963. pp. 9, 18, and 21.

20. Marion Milner: *An Experiment in Leisure*. Virago, 1986. p. 50.

21. Rollo May: *The Cry for Myth*. Souvenir Press, 1993. p. 9.

22. Ib., p. 49.

23. R.D. Laing: *The Politics of Experience*. Penguin, 1967. p. 116.

24. Ib., p. 136.

25. Don Cupitt: *The Sea of Faith*. B.B.C., 1984. p. 31.

26. C.G. Jung: *Modern Man in Search of a Soul*. Tr. W.S. Dell and Cary F. Baynes. Routledge & Kegan Paul, 1961. p. 130.

27. Joseph Campbell: *The Hero with a Thousand Faces*. Fontana, 1993. p. 257.

28. Mircea Eliade: *Images and Symbols*. Tr. Philip Mairet. Harvill Press, 1961. p. 11 (Italics mine).

29. Ib., p. 19.

30. E.F. Schumacher: *A Guide for the Perplexed*. Jonathan Cape,

1977. pp. 15 and 153.

31. E.F. Schumacher: *A Guide for the Perplexed*. Op. cit., p. 82.

32. C.G. Jung: *Modern Man in Search of a Soul*. Tr. R. F. C. Hull. Routledge & Kegan Paul, 1974. p. 264.

33. C.G. Jung: *Selected Writings*. Introduced by Anthony Storr. Fontana, 1983. pp. 260-261.

34. C.G. Jung: *Letters, Vol. II, 1951-1961*. Selected and edited by G. Adler in collaboration with Aniela Jaffe. Tr. R.F.C. Hull. R.K.P., 1976. pp. 74-77.

35. Karen Armstrong: *The Battle for God*. Op. cit., p. 201.

36. Ib., p. 144.

37. C.G. Jung: *The Undiscovered Self*. Op. cit., p. 64.

38. C.G. Jung: *The Integration of the Personality*. Tr. Stanley Dell. Routledge & Kegan Paul, 1940. p. 286.

39. Pierre Teilhard de Chardin: *The Future of Man*. Tr. Norman Denny. Collins, 1964. p. 303.

40. C.G. Jung: *The Undiscovered Self*. Op. cit., p. 63.

41. .C.G. Jung: *Answer to Job*. Routledge & Kegan Paul: Ark Paperbacks, 1984. p. 169.

42. C.G. Jung: *Memories, Dreams and Reflections*. Recorded and edited by Aniela Jaffe. Tr. Richard and Clare Winston. Collins Fontana, 1967. Note on p. 414.

43. Joseph Campbell: *The Hero with a Thousand Faces*. Op. cit., p. 11.

44. C.G. Jung: *Selected Writings*. Op. cit., p. 197.

45. Nikos Kazantzakis: *Report to Greco*. Bruno Cassirer, 1965. p. 483.

46. Ib., p. 15.

47. Deuteronomy 6: 5.

48. C.G. Jung: *Selected Writings*. Op. cit., p. 261.

Chapter 2

1. Luke 16: 19 – 31.

2. Robert Winston: *The Story of God*. Bantam Press/Random

House, 2005. p. 8.

3. Geza Vermes: *Christian Beginnings*. Allen Lane, 2012, p. 60.
4. Philip Pullman: *The Good Man Jesus and the Scoundrel Christ*. Canongate, 2010. p. 259.
5. C.G. Jung: *Selected Writings*. Op. cit., p. 247-248.
6. John Steinbeck: *"About Ed Ricketts"* in *The Log from the Sea of Cortez*. Heinemann, 1958. p. x.
7. Buddhist Scriptures: selected and translated by Edward Conze. Penguin Books, 1959. Introduction, pp. 11-12.
8. Galatians 2: 11 and 14.
9. John 4:7 – 30; Mark 7: 25 – 30; Luke 7: 2 – 10.
10. Ephesians 2: 14.
11. Joseph Campbell: *The Masks of God*: Occidental Mythology (1964). Souvenir Press, 2001. p. 347.
12. Martin Buber: *Moses – The Revelation and the Covenant*. Harper Torchbooks, 1958. p. 61.
13. Abraham Maslow: *Towards a Psychology of Being*. Reinhold, 1968. p. 46.
14. John 9: 25.
15. Geza Vermes: *Jesus the Jew*. Fontana Collins, 1976. p. 129.
16. 1 Samuel 16: 7.
17. 1 Samuel 17.
18. Psalm 118: 22.
19. Luke 20:17; Acts 4:11.
20. Geza Vermes: *Jesus the Jew*. Op. cit., p. 80.
21. Deuteronomy 18: 15.
22. Matthew 2: 16.
23. See Exodus 1: 15 - 2: 10.
24. Luke 1: 32.
25. Luke 24: 45.
26. Luke 24: 27.
27. Isaiah 44: 1.
28. Mark 1: 11. Compare John 1: 14.
29. Isaiah 42: 1.

30. John 5: 30.
31. Mark 14: 36.
32. Daniel 7: 13-14.
33. Mark 1: 15.
34. Luke 17: 21.
35. E.P. Sanders: *The Historical Figure of Jesus*. Penguin, 1995. p. 248.
36. John 10: 10.
37. Pierre Teilhard de Chardin: *The Future of Man*. Op. cit., p. 187.

Chapter 3

1. Karen Armstrong: *The Case for God*. The Bodley Head, 2009. p. 132 (italics mine).
2. Martin Palmer: *The Jesus Sutras*. Piatkus, 2001.
3. Victor White: *God and the Unconscious*. Fontana, 1960. p. 244
4. Dietrich Bonhoeffer: *Letters and Papers from Prison*. Ed. Eberhard Bethge. Abridged edition, S.C.M., 1981. p. 89.
5. Joseph Campbell: *The Hero with a Thousand Faces*. Op. cit., p. 389.
6. P.W. Martin: *Experiment in Depth*. Routledge & Kegan Paul, 1976. pp. 190-191.
7. Ib., p. 191.
8. Mark 1: 11.
9. John 1: 13.
10. Mark 1: 22.
11. Luke 18: 9-14.
12. Erich Fromm: *Beyond the Chains of Illusion*. Op. cit., p. 169.
13. Luke 15: 29-30.
14. Matthew 20: 1 – 16.
15. Matthew 6: 24.
16. Luke 11: 43; Matthew 23: 6 - 7; Mark 12: 38-39.
17. Matthew 6: 2, 5, and 16.
18. Erich Fromm: *To Have or To Be?* Jonathan Cape, 1978. pp. 109-

110.

19. Matthew 6: 19-21; Luke 12: 33-34.

20. Matthew 6: 25-34; Luke 12: 22-31.

21. Alan Richardson: *A Theological Word Book of the Bible*. SCM, 1957. p. 192.

22. Matthew 7: 1 and 5; Luke 6: 37 and 42.

23. Matthew 7: 18.

24. Luke 6: 45.

25. Matthew 13: 44-46.

26. John 1: 9.

27. Matthew 7: 7-8; Luke 11: 9-10.

28. Mark 8: 34-37.

29. Matthew 10:39 and 16: 25, Luke 9: 24 and 17: 33; John 12: 25.

30. Matthew 19: 29

31. Colin Turnbull: *The Human Cycle*. Jonathan Cape: Triad/Paladin Books, 1985. p. 102.

32. Anthony Stevens: *Private Myths: Dreams and Dreaming*. Penguin, 1996. p. 157.

33. Rollo May: *The Courage to Create*. Collins, 1976. p. 106.

34. Edward Schillebeeckx: *Jesus – An Experiment in Christology*. Tr. Hubert Hoskins. Collins, 1979. p. 157.

35. Ib., p. 169.

36. Martin Buber: *Hasidism and Modern Man*. Op. cit., pp. 42-43.

37. 2 Samuel 11: 26 – 12: 14.

38. J. Jeremias: *The Parables of Jesus*. Tr. S. H. Hooke. SCM, 1954. p. 19.

39. Luke 10: 25-37.

40. John 4: 9.

41. Luke 15: 1-2 and 11-32.

42. Martin Buber: *Between Man and Man*. Tr. R. Gregor Smith. Collins Fontana, 1961. p. 36.

43. Luke 6: 41.

44. Luke 16: 19-31 and 18: 9-14.

45. Geza Vermes: *Jesus the Jew*. Op. cit., p. 81.

46. Matthew 23: 13; Luke 11: 52.

47. William Blake: *The Garden of Love*.

48. Mark 10: 17-22.

49. Luke 12: 13.

50. Luke 12: 15.

51. Luke 12: 16-21 and 16: 19-31.

52. Mark 4: 3-9.

53. Mark 4: 17.

54. Mark 6: 2-3.

55. 1 Samuel 16: 1-13.

56. J. Jeremias: *The Parables of Jesus*. Op. cit., p. 19.

57. Matthew 22; 1-14. Compare Luke 14: 16-24.

58. Don Cupitt: *The Sea of Faith*. Op. cit., p. 247.

59. Charlie Pye-Smith: *Rebels and Outcasts*. Penguin, 1998.

60. Ib., p. 283.

61. Ib.

62. Ib. p. 284.

63. Geza Vermes: *Jesus the Jew*. Op.cit., p. 79.

64. Ib., p. 65.

65. Mark 6: 15; 9: 4; 15: 35.

66. Mark 8: 11-13; Matthew 12: 38-39; Luke 11: 29.

67. E.P. Sanders: *The Historical Figure of Jesus*. Op. cit., p. 167.

68. Barnabas Lindars: *The Gospel of John*. Marshall and Morgan Scott, 1981. p.239.

69. John 11: 43.

70. I Corinthians 15: 3-4.

71. Luke 24: 44-45.

72. Mark 13: 2.

73. E.P. Sanders. *The Historical Figure of Jesus*. Op. cit., p. 260.

74. Ib., p. 265.

75. John 11: 50.

76. E.P. Sanders: *The Historical Figure of Jesus*. Op. cit., p. 280.

77. 1 Corinthians 15: 5-8.

78. Mark 16: 5 - 6. (Verses 9 onwards are a later addition.)

79. C.F. Evans: *Saint Luke*. S.C.M. and Trinity Press International, 1980. p. 887.
80. Hans Küng: *On Being a Christian Today*. Tr. Edward Quinn. Image Books/Doubleday, 1976. p. 364.
81. Luke 24: 5
82. John 20: 17.
83. 2 Corinthians 5: 16.
84. Geza Vermes: *The Resurrection*. Penguin, 2008. P. 152.
85. Edward Schillebeeckx: Op. cit., p. 391.
86. Acts 1: 5.
87. Acts 1: 9.
88. 2 Kings 2: 9-12.
89. Acts 2: 2-4.
90. John 20: 21-22.
91. Joseph Campbell: *The Hero with a Thousand Faces*. Op. cit., p. 249.
92. Romans 6: 3-4.
93. Jacob Needleman: *Lost Christianity*. Element Books, 1990. p. 189.
94. Robin Skynner: *The Process of Growth* in W. Barlow (ed): *More Talk of Alexander*. Gollancz, 1978. p. 135.
95. Joseph Campbell: *The Hero with a Thousand Faces*. Op. cit., p. 104.

Chapter 4

1. Pierre Teilhard de Chardin: *The Future of Man*. Op. cit., p. 72.
2. Adrian Hastings: *Church and Mission in Modern Africa*. Burns & Oates, 1967. p. 141.
3. John 12: 24.
4. John 12: 25; Mark 8: 35; Matthew 10: 39 and 16: 25; Luke 9: 24 and 17: 33.
5. Luke 2: 46.
6. Luke 24: 45.
7. Galatians 3: 28

8. Luke 2: 32.

9. Hebrews 11: 8.

10 Genesis 32: 28.

11 Hebrews 11: 27.

12. Hebrews 11: 34.

13. Matthew 25: 34-36.

14. Isaiah 58: 6-7.

15. Theodore Roszak: *The Cult of Information*. Lutterworth Press, 1986. p.214.

16. Bede Griffiths: *Return to the Centre*. Collins, 1976. p. 110.

17. Karen Armstrong: *The Case for God*. Op. cit., p. 308.

18. Rudolf Otto: *The Idea of the Holy*. Tr. John W. Harvey. OUP, 1923. pp. 67-8.

19. Geza Vermes: *Christian Beginnings*. Op. cit.

20. John 1: 12.

21. Romans 8: 14 – 17 and 29.

22. Marion Milner: *An Experiment in Leisure*. Op. Cit., p. 135.

23. Nicolas Berdyaev: *Freedom and Spirit*. Op. cit., p. 268.

24. Evelyn Underhill: *Mysticism*. (1910) Oneworld, Oxford, 1999. p. 425.

25. John V. Taylor: *The Christlike God*. SCM, 1992. p. 275.

26. Luke 5: 16.

27. Luke 6; 12.

28. Luke 11: 1.

29. Matthew 6: 6.

30. Romans 8: 15 - 16.

31. Romans 8: 15.

32. C.G. Jung: Letters. Vol 2, 1951 – 1961. Op. cit., page 28.

33. John 8: 32.

34. Peter Vardy: *Being Human*. Darton, Longman and Todd, 2003. p. 100.

35. Matthew 7: 14. Compare Luke 13: 24.

36. Luke 11: 2.

37. Alan Paton: *Towards the Mountain*. Oxford University Press,

1980. p. 253 (Italics mine).

38. The Guardian, March 23, 2010.

39. Mark 14: 36.

40. Matthew 4: 1-11; Luke 4: 1-13.

41. Exodus 16.

42. Luke 22: 12-24; Matthew 6: 25-26.

43. Viktor E. Frankl: *Man's Search for Meaning*. Tr. Ilse Lasch. Op. cit., p. 86.

44. Robert Macfarlane: *The Wild Places*. Granta Books, 2008. p. 236.

45. W.H. Auden: *A Selection by the Author*. Penguin, 1958. p. 69.

46. C.G. Jung: *Modern Man in Search of a Soul*. Op. cit., p. 272.

47. C.G. Jung: *Selected Writings*. Op. cit., pp. 242-243.

48. Luke 6: 42; Matthew 7: 4.

49. Thomas Merton: *The Hidden Ground of Love*. Farrar, Strauss, Giroux, 1985. p. 53.

50. Mark 8: 33.

51. Nikos Kazantzakis: *Report to Greco*. Op. cit., p. 496.

52. Joseph Campbell: *The Hero with a Thousand Faces*. Op. cit., p. 337.

53. C.G. Jung: *Letters, Vol. 1, 1906-1950*. Edited by G. Adler in collaboration with Aniela Jaffe, tr. R.F.C. Hull. Routledge & Kegan Paul, 1973. p. 387.

54. Thomas Merton: *The Intimate Merton*. Edited by Patrick Hart and Jonathan Montaldo. Lion Publishing, 2000. p. 42.

55. T.S. Eliot: *The Wasteland and Other Poems*. Faber and Faber, 1971. p. 72

56. T.S. Eliot: *Murder in the Cathedral*. Faber and Faber, 1961. pp. 9 and 10.

57. John 4: 14.

Conclusion

1. John Hick: *The Fifth Dimension*. Op. cit., p. 238.

2. Hugh Brody: *Maps and Dreams*. Faber, 1986.

3. Ib., p. 45-46.

4. Mircea Eliade: *Images and Symbols*. Op. cit., p. 12.

5. Ib., p. 20.

6. Ib., p. 59 (Italics in original).

7. C.G. Jung: *Memories, Dreams and Reflections*. Op. cit., p. 373.

8. Philip Pullman. *The Good Man Jesus and the Scoundrel Christ*. Op. cit., p. 252.

9. Buddhist Scriptures. Selected and translated by Edward Conze. Op. cit., pp. 35 and 63.

10. John 12: 24

11. Matthew 6: 6.

12. Thomas Merton: *Contemplation in a World of Action*. Geo. Allen and Unwin, 1971. p. 347.

13. C.G. Jung: *Selected Writings*. Op. cit., p. 248-9.

14. Richard Holloway: *Doubts and Loves*. Canongate, 2001. p. 16.

15. John Hick: *The Non-Absoluteness of Christianity* in *The Myth of Christian Uniqueness*. Ed. John Hick and Paul F. Knitter. SCM, 1987. p. 26.

16. The Koran. Tr. and with an Introduction by Arthur J. Arberry. Oxford University Press, 1998. XLII: 14, p. 500.

Bibliography

ADLER, Alfred   *Understanding Human Nature.* Tr. Colin Brett. Oneworld, Oxford, 1998.

ARMSTRONG, Karen *A History of God.* Vintage, 1999.
The Battle for God. Fundamentalism in Judaism, Christianity and Islam. Harper Collins, 2000.
A Short History of Myth. Canongate, 2005.
The Case for God. The Bodley Head, 2009.

AUDEN, W. H.   *A Selection by the Author.* Penguin, 1958.

BERDYAEV, N.   *Freedom and Spirit.* Tr. Oliver Fielding Clarke. Geoffrey Bles: Centenary Press, 1935.

BONHOEFFER, Dietrich. *Letters and Papers from Prison.* Ed. Eberhard Bethge. Abridged Edition. SCM, 1981.

BRODY, Hugh.   *Maps and Dreams.* Faber, 1986.

BUBER, Martin.   *Hasidism and Modern Man.* Tr. Maurice Friedman. Harper Torchbooks, 1958.
Moses – The Revelation and the Covenant. Harper Torchbooks, 1958.
Between Man and Man. Tr. R. Gregor Smith. Collins Fontana, 1961.

BUDDHIST SCRIPTURES Selected and translated by Edward Conze. Penguin, 1959.

BYRON, Robert.   *The Station.* Century Publishing, 1984.

CAMPBELL, Joseph. *The Masks of God: Occidental Mythology.* (1964) Souvenir Press, 2001.

	The Hero with a Thousand Faces. Fontana, 1993.
CUPITT, Don.	*The Sea of Faith.* BBC, 1984.
DAWKINS, Richard.	*The God Delusion.* Bantam, 2006.
	Unweaving the Rainbow. Penguin, 1998.
ELIADE, Mircea.	*Images and Symbols.* Tr. Philip Mairet. Harvill Press, 1961.
ELIOT, T. S.	*Murder in the Cathedral.* Faber and Faber, 1961.
	The Wasteland and Other Poems. Faber and Faber,1971.
EVANS, C. F.	*Saint Luke.* SCM and Trinity Press International, 1980.
FRANKL, Viktor E.	*Man's Search for Meaning.* Tr. Ilse Lasch. Hodder and Stoughton, 1987.
	Man's Search for Ultimate Meaning. Insight Books: Plenum Press, New York, 1997.
FRAZER, James G.	*Introduction to Apollodorus: The Library.* Heinemann, 1921.
FREUD, Sigmund.	*The Future of an Illusion.* Hogarth Press, 1961.
	Civilisation and its Discontents. Hogarth Press, 1963.
FROMM, Erich	*Psychoanalysis and Religion.* Yale University Press, 1950.
	To Have or To Be? Jonathan Cape, 1978.
	Beyond the Chains of Illusion. Abacus, 1980.
GRIFFITHS, Bede.	*Return to the Centre.* Collins, 1976.
HASTINGS, Adrian.	*Church and Mission in Modern Africa.* Burns & Oates, 1967.

HICK, John.   *The Non-Absoluteness of Christianity* in *The Myth of Christian Uniqueness.* Ed. John Hick and Paul F. Knitter. SCM, 1987.

The Fifth Dimension. Oneworld, Oxford, 1999

HOLLOWAY, Richard.   *Doubts and Loves.* Canongate, 2001.

IYER, Rhagavan (Ed.). *The Moral and Political Writings of Mahatma Gandhi.*Vol. 1. Oxford University Press, 1986.

JEREMIAS, J.   *The Parables of Jesus.* Tr. S. H. Hooke. SCM, 1954.

JUNG, C. G.   *The Integration of the Personality.* Tr. Stanley Dell. Routledge & Kegan Paul, 1940.

Modern Man in Search of a Soul. Tr. W.S.Dell and Cary F. Baynes. Routledge & Kegan Paul, 1961.

Memories, Dreams and Reflections. Recorded and edited by Aniela Jaffe. Tr. Richard and Clare Winston. Collins Fontana, 1967.

Letters, Vol. I, 1906 – 1950. Edited by G. Adler in collaboration with Aniela Jaffe. Tr. R. F. C. Hull. Routledge & Kegan Paul, 1973.

The Undiscovered Self. Tr. R. F. C. Hull. Routledge & Kegan Paul, 1974.

Letters, Vol. II, 1951 – 1961. Selected and edited by G. Adler in collaboration with Aniela Jaffe. Tr. R. F. C. Hull. Routledge & Kegan Paul, 1976.

Selected Writings. Introduced by Anthony Storr. Fontana, 1983.

	Answer to Job. Routledge & Kegan Paul: Ark Paperbacks, 1984.
KAZANTZAKIS, Nikos.	*Report to Greco.* Bruno Cassirer, 1965.
KORAN, The.	Tr. and Introduction by Arthur J. Arberry. Oxford University Press, 1998.
KŰNG, Hans.	*On Being a Christian Today.* Tr. Edward Quinn. Image Books/Doubleday, 1976.
LAING, R. D.	*The Politics of Experience.* Penguin, 1967.
LINDARS, Barnabas.	*The Gospel of John.* Marshall and Morgan Scott, 1981.
MACFARLANE, Robert.	*The Wild Places.* Granta Books, 2008.
MARTIN, P.W.	*Experiment in Depth.* Routledge & Kegan Paul, 1976.
MARX, Karl.	*Towards a Critique of Hegel's Philosophy of Right.* Cited in E. Fromm: *Beyond the Chains of Illusion.* Abacus, 1980.
MASLOW, Abraham.	*Towards a Psychology of Being.* Reinhold, 1968.
MAY, Rollo.	*The Cry for Myth.* Souvenir Press, 1993.
	The Courage to Create. Collins, 1976.
MERTON, Thomas.	*Contemplation in a World of Action.* Geo. Allen and Unwin, 1971.
	The Hidden Ground of Love. Farrar, Strauss, Giroux, 1985.
MILNER, Marion.	*An Experiment in Leisure.* Virago, 1986.
MUMFORD, Lewis.	*My Works and Days.* Harcourt Brace Jovanovich, 1980.
NEEDLEMAN, Jacob.	*Lost Christianity.* Element Books, 1990.
OTTO, Rudolf.	*The Idea of the Holy* Tr. John W. Harvey. OUP, 1923..

PALMER, Martin. *The Jesus Sutras*. Piatkus, 2001.

PATON, Alan. *Towards the Mountain*. Oxford University Press, 1980.

PYE-SMITH, Charlie. *Rebels and Outcasts*. Penguin, 1998.

PULLMAN. Philip. *The Good Man Jesus and the Scoundrel Christ*. Canongate, 2010.

RICHARDSON, Alan. *A Theological Word Book of the Bible*. SCM, 1957.

ROSZAK, Theodore. *Where the Wasteland Ends*. Anchor Doubleday, 1973.
The Cult of Information. Lutterworth Press, 1986.

SANDERS, E.P. *The Historical Figure of Jesus*. Penguin, 1995.

SCHILLEBEECKX, E. *Jesus – An Experiment in Christology*. Tr. Hubert Hoskins. Collins, 1979.

SCHUMACHER, E. F. *A Guide for the Perplexed*. Jonathan Cape, 1977.

SKYNNER, Robin. *The Process of Growth*. In W. Barlow (ed.): *More Talk of Alexander*. Gollancz, 1978.

STEINBECK, John. *"About Ed Ricketts"* in *The Log from the Sea of Cortez*. Heinemann, 1958.

STEVENS, Anthony. *Private Myths: Dreams and Dreaming*. Penguin, 1996.

TAYLOR, John V. *The Christlike God*. SCM, 1992.

TEILHARD DE *The Future of Man*. Tr. Norman Denny. Collins, 1964.

CHARDIN, Pierre.

TURNBULL, Colin. *The Human Cycle*. Jonathan Cape: Triad/Paladin Books, 1985.

UNDERHILL, Evelyn. *Mysticism* (1910). Oneworld, Oxford, 1999.

VARDY, Peter. *Being Human*. Darton, Longman and

	Todd, 2003.
VERMES,Geza.	*Christian Beginnings.* Allen Lane, 2012.
	Jesus the Jew. Fontana Collins, 1976.
	The Resurrection. Penguin, 2008.
WHITE, Victor.	*God and the Unconscious.* Fontana, 1960.
WINSTON, Robert	*The Story of God.* Bantam Press/ Random House, 2005.

CHRISTIAN
ALTERNATIVE

Throughout the two thousand years of Christian tradition there have been, and still are, groups and individuals that exist in the margins and upon the edge of faith. But in Christianity's contrapuntal history it has often been these outcasts and pioneers that have forged contemporary orthodoxy out of former radicalism as belief evolves to engage with and encompass the ever-changing social and scientific realities. Real faith lies not in the comfortable certainties of the Orthodox, but somewhere in a half-glimpsed hinterland on the dirt track to Emmaus, where the Death of God meets the Resurrection, where the supernatural Christ meets the historical Jesus, and where the revolution liberates both the oppressed and the oppressors.

Welcome to Christian Alternative... a space at the edge where the light shines through.